WHAT
HAPPENED
TO THE
CROSS?

WHAT
HAPPENED
TO THE
CROSS?

Distinctive LDS Teachings

ROBERT L. MILLET

DESERET
BOOK
SALT LAKE CITY, UTAH

Library of Congress Cataloging-in-Publication Data

Millet, Robert L.
  What happened to the cross? : distinctive LDS teachings /
Robert L. Millet.
      p. cm.
  Includes bibliographical references and index.
  ISBN-13: 978-1-59038-789-4 (hardback : alk. paper)
  1. Church of Jesus Christ of Latter-day Saints. 2. Mormon Church. 3. Jesus Christ—Mormon interpretations. I. Title.
  BX8635.3.M56 2007
  230'.9332—dc22   2007025602

Printed in the United States of America
Sheridan Books Inc., Ann Arbor, MI

10   9   8   7   6   5   4   3   2   1

To Robert J. Matthews

Teacher, mentor, leader, colleague, and treasured friend

True doctrine, understood, changes attitudes and behavior. The study of the doctrines of the gospel will improve behavior quicker than a study of behavior will improve behavior. . . . That is why we stress so forcefully the study of the doctrines of the gospel.

BOYD K. PACKER

CONTENTS

ACKNOWLEDGMENTS

No book of this type arrives at the point of publication without the careful and painstaking attention of many, many people. I express my sincere gratitude to the entire Deseret Book staff, who have been patient but direct, kindly but insistent on shaping the submitted manuscript into a much better book. I am particularly indebted to my editor and friend, Suzanne Brady, whose insightful suggestions and close reading of the text have created a project that we all feel better about. As ever, I am grateful to my supportive and encouraging wife, Shauna, whose commitment to the faith, quiet, steady discipleship, and spontaneous charity have created an atmosphere of peace conducive to thinking and writing about eternal things.

LAYING THE DOCTRINAL FOUNDATION

"Beware of false prophets," the Savior warned in the meridian of time, "which come to you in sheep's clothing, but inwardly they are ravening wolves. *Ye shall know them by their fruits.* Do men gather grapes of thorns, or figs of thistles? Even so every good tree bringeth forth good fruit; but a corrupt tree bringeth forth evil fruit. . . . Wherefore by their fruits ye shall know them" (Matthew 7:15–17, 20; emphasis added).

If we were to apply this standard of judgment to Joseph Smith and the work he helped to set in motion, we might ask, What are the fruits of Mormonism? What difference does conversion to The Church of Jesus Christ of Latter-day Saints make? How does our religious tradition and way of life affect our day-to-day walk and talk? How would it change society if the entire world adopted it? As Latter-day Saints and thus followers of Joseph Smith, we might well point to the profound effect the Church has on personal spirituality, families, loyal citizenship, absolute values, unchanging moral standards, health, the care of the poor, or the education of its members. These are all fruits of the faith, evidences that the seed planted in 1830 is a good seed, one that is bringing forth beautiful and tasty fruit.

There is, however, a fruit of the Restoration that is too easily slighted. Indeed, it is a fruit that underlies all the good and noble and uplifting products of our faith: it is our doctrine, our theology. In a Regional Representatives Seminar in April 1981, Elder Bruce R. McConkie gave the following parable:

"Hear now the parable of the unwise builder:

"A certain man inherited a choice piece of ground whereon to build a house to shelter his loved ones from the storms of the day and the cold of the night.

"He began his work with zeal and skill, using good materials, for the need was urgent.

"But in his haste, and because he gave no heed to the principles of proper construction, he laid no foundation, but commencing immediately, he built the floor, and raised the walls, and began to cover them with a roof.

"Then, to his sorrow, because his house had no foundation, it fell and became a heap of rubble, and those whom he loved had no shelter.

"Verily, verily, I say unto you: A wise builder, when he buildeth a house, first layeth the foundation and then buildeth thereon.

"Hear now the interpretation of the parable of the unwise builder:

"A certain Church officer was called to build a house of faith and righteousness and salvation for the souls entrusted to his care. Knowing he had been called by inspiration and having great zeal, he hastened to strengthen and build up the programs of the Church without first laying the foundation of faith and testimony and conversion.

"He spent his time on mechanics and means and programs and procedures and teaching leadership and never laid the great and eternal foundation upon which all things must rest in the Lord's house—the foundation of our theology and our doctrine.

"I am told," Elder McConkie continued, "that a high Catholic prelate said to one who held the holy apostleship: 'There are two things which you Mormons have which we as Catholics would like to adopt.'

" 'What are they?' he was asked.

" 'They are tithing and your missionary system,' he replied.

" 'Well, why don't you adopt them?' came the rejoinder.

" 'We would except for two reasons: our people won't pay tithing, and our people won't go on missions.'

"How often have well-meaning and sincere people in the world attempted to adopt our youth programs, our family home evening program, our missionary system, and so on, and yet have not been able to operate them in their situations!

"Why? Because they do not lay a proper foundation; however inspired the programs may be, they do not stand alone. They must be built on the foundation of faith and doctrine.

"The foundation upon which we build our whole Church system is one of testimony and faith and conversion. It is our theology; it is the doctrine God has given us in this day; it is the restored and revealed principles of eternal truth—these are the things that give us the ability to operate our programs and build houses of salvation."[1]

What do we mean when we stand and bear witness that Joseph Smith was and is a prophet of God, the Prophet of the Restoration, the head of the dispensation of the fulness of times? First of all, it means that Joseph Smith was a legal administrator, one empowered by God through the ministration of heavenly beings, one upon whom divine priesthood authority was bestowed, one called to reestablish the Church and kingdom of God and oversee the performance of saving ordinances. "Whenever men can find out the will of God," Brother Joseph taught, "and find an administrator legally authorized from God, there is the kingdom of God; but where these are not, the kingdom of God is not. All the ordinances, systems, and administrations on the earth are of no use to the children of men, unless they are ordained and authorized of God; for nothing will save a man but a legal administrator; for none others will be acknowledged either by God or angels."[2] Truly, "there is no salvation between the two lids of the Bible without a legal administrator."[3]

Of equal importance, Joseph Smith is a prophet of God in the sense that he was a revealer of truth, one called to make known the God of heaven and the eternal plan of salvation. Prophets are men who have the testimony of Jesus (Revelation 19:10), men charged to bear that testimony by precept and example. From modern revelation we learn that prophets are those called to bear apostolic testimony, to stand boldly as special witnesses of the name of Christ in all the world (D&C 107:23). They are charged to declare and clarify and elucidate and correct and expand upon doctrinal matters. President Gordon B. Hinckley was asked in an interview by Larry King, "You're the leader of a major religion. What's your role?" President Hinckley responded: "*My role is to declare doctrine.* My role is to stand as an example before the people. *My role is to be a voice in defense of the truth.* My role is to stand as a conservator of those values which are important in our civilization and our society. My role is to lead."[4]

It has been my privilege and honor to work for more than three decades with the youth of the Church in seminary, institute, and university. These marvelous young people are great ambassadors of our faith—but not simply because they refrain from smoking or drinking or because they dress modestly. Those characteristics are indeed impressive, but they are the evidence, the manifestation, of something much deeper within them. They act and look great because of their faith and witness, because of what they believe. What we believe determines what we do, who we are, and what we become.

Our entire system of ethics—what we do and what we do not do—is built upon the doctrines of salvation. The pattern is set in scripture: God gave commandments to the ancients *after* he had made known the plan of redemption (Alma 12:32). Elder Boyd K. Packer has taught: "True doctrine, understood, changes attitudes and behavior. The study of the doctrines of the gospel will improve behavior quicker than a study of behavior will improve behavior. . . . That is why we stress so forcefully the study of the doctrines of the gospel."[5]

"Doctrines believed and practiced do change and improve us," Elder Neal A. Maxwell pointed out, "while ensuring our vital access to the Spirit. Both outcomes are crucial."[6]

In that spirit, with our eyes focused forevermore on the Savior and our hearts turned reverently to his infinite and eternal sacrifice, we entitle this book *What Happened to the Cross?* As discussed in chapter 6, the cross has become for the Christian world a symbol of the Atonement, a reminder and representation of the most significant event—and thus the most powerful doctrine—in all eternity. The gospel of Jesus Christ is the message of the Atonement, the good news or glad tidings that redemption from the Fall and the strength to live abundantly and victoriously have come into the world in and through the Person and the work of Jesus the Christ (John 10:10; D&C 76:40–42). Joseph Smith was called to reveal Christ anew. The Restoration that began with the Prophet is a re-revelation of the message of salvation, a modern declaration of "Jesus Christ, and him crucified" (1 Corinthians 2:2). The dispensation of the fulness of times is an era in which all the streams and rivers of past revelation flow wondrously into the ocean of restored truth, as well as a season when things never before revealed have been and will yet be revealed (Article of Faith 9).

After the Mesa Arizona Temple was renovated a number of years ago, President Gordon B. Hinckley observed: "Clergy of other religions were invited to tour it on the first day of the open house period. Hundreds responded. In speaking to them, I said we would be pleased to answer any queries they might have. Among these was one from a Protestant minister.

"Said he: 'I've been all through this building, this temple which carries on its face the name of Jesus Christ, but nowhere have I seen any representation of the cross, the symbol of Christianity. I have noted your buildings elsewhere and likewise find an absence of the cross. Why is this when you say you believe in Jesus Christ?'

"I responded: 'I do not wish to give offense to any of my Christian colleagues who use the cross on the steeples of their cathedrals and at the altars of their chapels, who wear it on their vestments, and imprint it on their books and other literature. But for us, the cross is the symbol of the dying Christ, while our message is a declaration of the Living Christ.'

"He then asked: 'If you do not use the cross, what is the symbol of your religion?'

"I replied that the lives of our people must become the most meaningful expression of our faith and, in fact, therefore, the symbol of our worship.'"[7]

In other words, the question "What happened to the cross?" could be restated for our purposes here as "How have we applied our doctrine?" What we believe always affects how we live. And so, this is a book about several distinctive doctrines of the Restoration, those sweet and sublime teachings that rivet our souls on Christ, who is the Center.

While we rejoice in modern revelation, that God continues to make known his mind and will through living oracles today, we readily acknowledge that most of the doctrines, most of the principles and divine statutes that have been delivered to the Latter-day Saints, have come through the instrumentality of Joseph Smith.

When asked how revelations come through the leaders of the Church, President Hinckley stated: "Let me say first that *we have a great body of revelations, the vast majority of which came from the Prophet Joseph Smith.* We don't need much revelation. We need to pay more attention to the revelation we have already received. But we have that background and nearly every problem with which we deal, we deal with it on the basis of that revelation we have."[8]

But occasionally things arise, he explained to Mike Wallace, "where the will of the Lord [is needed and] is sought, and in those circumstances I think the best way I could describe the process is to liken it to the experience of Elijah as set forth in the book of First Kings [19:9–12]." After describing the influence of the still, small voice, President Hinckley testified: "Now, let me just say, categorically, that the things of God are understood by the Spirit of God, and one must have and seek and cultivate that Spirit, and there comes understanding and it is real. I can give testimony of that."[9]

Early in his ministry, the Prophet Joseph was instructed concerning both dimensions of his prophetic office: "In temporal labors thou shalt not have strength, for this is not thy calling. Attend to thy calling and thou shalt have wherewith to magnify thine office, and *to expound all scriptures,* and continue in laying on of the hands and confirming the churches" (D&C 24:9; emphasis added). The early Saints were similarly told to "teach one another the doctrine of the kingdom. Teach ye diligently and my grace shall attend you" (D&C 88:77–78). Like his Master, the Prophet Joseph Smith was first and foremost a teacher, a revealer of truth, a mouthpiece of God, one chosen from before the foundation of the world to gaze upon the scenes of eternity and then invite others to share with him in the fruits and enjoyment of that vision.

CHAPTER ONE

---◦◦◦---

IN THE SPRING OF 1820

Latter-day Saints are called upon to walk a fine line. On the one hand, we have been encouraged to reach out to persons of other faiths, to strive to build friendships and lasting relationships, to work together with men and women of good will to identify and stand against growing evils in our world. Latter-day Saints are Christian, to be sure, and it matters very much to us that others understand that. But the differences between us begin with the spring of 1820.

The War of Words

Although Catholicism claims apostolic succession—that the bishops of the ancient church conveyed their priesthood powers from the bishop of Rome down to the Pope in our time—God's divine authority was not to be found in the Old World by the middle of the second century after Christ and in the New World by the middle of the fifth century after Christ. The Roman Church had control of the Christian faith until a split took place in 1054, resulting in the creation of the Eastern Orthodox faiths. In the West during the fifteenth and sixteenth centuries courageous individuals objected to, opposed, and eventually broke away from Catholicism. Through such persons as John Hus, Martin Luther, John Calvin, Roger Williams, John Wesley, and others, what we know as the Protestant Reformation came to pass. The Reformers emphasized the need to turn to scripture for authority—that is, *sola scriptura* ("scripture alone")—as well as such matters as the complete sovereignty of God, the total depravity of man, and salvation by grace alone. Further, sickened by the abuses of a priestly hierarchy, the Protestants emphasized a "priesthood of all believers." Followers of John Calvin believed in what came to be known as the "five points of Calvinism," doctrines that may be conveniently listed under the acronym TULIP:

- *T*otal depravity (men and women are fallen and lost; their works are useless and as "filthy rags")
- *U*nconditional election (predestination)
- *L*imited atonement (only for those who are the elect)
- *I*rresistibility of grace (one cannot escape one's election to salvation)
- *P*erseverance of the saints (one cannot fall from grace).

In contrast, followers of Jacob Arminius, who came to be known as Arminians, took issue with Calvin. They believed in the power of human will and opposed those doctrines associated with predestination. One Arminian, John Wesley, became the father of Methodism.

These ideas, only sketched here, provide the background and setting for the First Vision. Joseph Smith recalled his dilemma: "My mind at times was greatly excited, the cry and tumult were so great and incessant. The Presbyterians were most decided against the Baptists and Methodists, and used all the powers of both reason and sophistry to prove their errors, or, at least, to make the people think they were in error. On the other hand, the Baptists and Methodists in their turn were equally zealous in endeavoring to establish their own tenets and disprove all others.

"In the midst of this war of words and tumult of opinions, I often said to myself: What is to be done? Who of all these parties are right; or, are they all wrong together? If any one of them be right, which is it, and how shall I know it?" (Joseph Smith–History 1:9–10).

I am indebted to my friend and colleague Professor Milton V. Backman Jr. for the following summary of doctrinal beliefs at the time of the First Vision, which assists us to better appreciate what the Prophet meant when he spoke of the "war of words and tumult of opinions."[1]

Baptism

Presbyterians, Methodists, Congregationalists, and Episcopalians believed that infants were proper subjects of baptism and that sprinkling, pouring, and immersion were proper modes of baptism.

Baptists and Eastern Christians held that only believers should be baptized and that immersion was the only correct mode of baptism.

The Society of Friends, or Quakers, rejected all sacraments.

Man's Role in the Experience of Salvation

Calvinist Baptists (including the Baptists of Palmyra and Manchester, New York), Presbyterians, and Congregationalists believed in the Five Points of Calvinism.

Methodists, Freewill Baptists, Quakers, and Episcopalians believed in Arminianism: Man depraved (but not totally), God's foreknowledge (but not predestination), limited atonement (all believers who persevere to the end benefit from the Atonement), man can reject the call, and man can fall.

Sources of Religious Truth

Baptists, Presbyterians, Methodists, Congregationalists, Episcopalians, and Eastern Christians held that the Bible was the sole source of truth and standard of faith. Most also held that the Bible was without error or flaw.

Quakers believed that the primary source of religious truth was latter-day revelation, contending that the Bible contained errors of omission, additions, and mistranslations.

Godhead

Baptists, Presbyterians, Congregationalists, Episcopalians, and Quakers believed in the Trinity, the triune God consisting of three persons of one essence, substance, or being.

Eastern Christians, most Unitarians, and Universalists held that the Father and Son were separate and distinct spirits.

Authority

Baptists, Presbyterians, Methodists, Congregationalists, and Eastern Christians accepted the notion of a priesthood of all believers.

Catholics and Episcopalians believed in apostolic succession.

Quakers held that there was no need for authority (no sacraments or ordinances).

Life beyond the Grave

Baptists, Presbyterians, Methodists, Episcopalians, Eastern Christians, and Quakers believed in a heaven and hell.

Universalists and most Unitarians believed in universal salvation, the idea that everyone would eventually go to heaven.

THE FIRST VISION—MESSAGE AND SIGNIFICANCE

Camp meetings and revivals were held frequently throughout what came to be known as the Burnt-Over District. At the time of the First Vision only about 11 percent of the people in this nation and in the immediate vicinity of where Joseph Smith lived were members of a Christian organization. There are more reports of revivals in upstate and western New York in 1819 and 1820 than in any other section of the country. In his 1838 account of the First Vision (in the Pearl of Great Price), the Prophet did not state that great multitudes were joining churches just in Palmyra but rather in the whole region or district or country. Methodism was the fastest growing religion in America at the time; the Methodists held more camp meetings than any other group.[2]

A number of timeless lessons may be learned from Joseph Smith's First Vision, including the following:

The Power of Pondering

One tradition holds that young Joseph Smith heard Reverend George Lane encourage seekers to "ask of God" and that James 1:5–6 was a part of some of his sermons.[3] There is no more moving and instructive statement of the power of pondering than that contained in the Prophet's words: "I was one day reading the Epistle of James, first chapter and fifth verse, which reads: If any of you lack wisdom, let him ask of God, which giveth to all men liberally, and upbraideth not; and it shall be given him.

"Never did any passage of scripture come with more power to the heart of man than this did at this time to mine. It seemed to enter with great force into every feeling of my heart. I reflected on it again and again, knowing that if any person needed wisdom from God, I did; for how to act I did not know, and unless I could get more wisdom than I then had, I would never know" (Joseph Smith–History 1:11–12).

Note the elements of pondering and meditation in this scenario: Joseph reflected on the scriptural words again and again; he had confidence in the word of God; and thus his was no superficial inquiry. He obviously had been taught by his parents that Holy Writ has eternal relevance. Young Joseph took an idea, a phrase written sometime around A.D. 50, and "likened" it to himself; he read James's words in their New Testament context and sensed that they had specific application to a farm boy in 1820 in upstate New York. "The Spirit of God rested mightily upon him. Not even Enoch and Abraham and Moses and the ancient prophets had been overpowered by such yearnings for truth and salvation as then filled Joseph's soul. As guided from on high, he retired to the place before appointed by the Lord of heaven and there began to offer up to God the desires of his heart."[4]

The Reality of Satan

A vital lesson to be learned by Joseph Smith early in his prophetic training was painful and poignant but one he would need to understand clearly: the reality of Satan and his eternal hatred for God and His plan of salvation. It was as though the father of lies sensed that he needed to confront Joseph Smith early and directly to attempt to stop the marvelous work and a wonder before it had a chance to get off the ground. Joseph explained that after he had knelt in the grove to offer up the yearnings of his soul, he "was seized upon by some power which entirely overcame me, and had such an astonishing influence over me as to bind my tongue so that I could not speak. Thick darkness gathered around me, and it seemed to me for a time as if I were doomed to sudden destruction" (Joseph Smith–History 1:15).

We have four accounts of the First Vision that Joseph Smith dictated: one in 1832, another in 1835, a third in 1838, and finally the account found in the 1842 Wentworth Letter.[5] In his 1835 account of the First Vision, the Prophet related that "information was what I most desired at this time, and with a fixed determination to obtain it, I called on the Lord for the first time in the place above stated, or in other words, I made a fruitless attempt to pray. My tongue seemed to be swollen in my mouth, so that I could not utter. I heard a noise behind me like some one walking towards me. I strove again to pray, but could not; the noise of walking seemed to draw nearer. I sprang upon my feet and looked around, but saw no person or thing that was calculated to produce the noise of walking. I kneeled again. My mouth was opened and my tongue loosed; I called on the Lord in mighty prayer. A pillar of fire appeared above my head, which presently rested down upon me, and filled me with unspeakable joy. A personage appeared in the midst of this pillar of flame, which was spread all around and yet nothing consumed. Another personage soon appeared like unto the first. He said unto me, 'Thy sins are forgiven thee.' He testified also unto me that Jesus Christ is the Son of God. I saw many angels in this vision. I was about 14 years old when I received this first communication."[6]

The Greater Power of God

Although Joseph became aware at an early age of the unspeakable power of the arch deceiver—an "actual being from the unseen world, who had such marvelous power as I had never before felt in any being" (Joseph Smith–History 1:16)—he also learned by firsthand experience that the power of God Almighty is greater. He is the Omnipotent One, the God of Glory (Moses 1:20).

In the first published account of the First Vision (1840, in Scotland), Elder Orson Pratt described the First Vision as follows:

"And while thus pouring out his soul, anxiously desiring an answer from God, he at length, saw a very bright and glorious light in the heavens above; which, at first, seemed to be a considerable distance. He continued praying, while the light appeared to be gradually descending towards him; and as it drew nearer, it increased in brightness and magnitude, so that, by the time that it reached the tops of the trees, the whole wilderness, for some distance around was illuminated in a most glorious and brilliant manner. He expected to have seen the leaves and boughs of the trees consumed, as soon as the light came in contact with them; but perceiving that it did not produce that effect, he was encouraged with the hope of being able to endure its presence."[7]

In the Wentworth Letter (1842), Joseph pointed out that "while fervently engaged in supplication, my mind was taken away from the objects with which I was surrounded, and I was enwrapped in a heavenly vision and saw two glorious personages who exactly resembled each other in features and likeness, surrounded with a brilliant light which eclipsed the sun at noon day."[8]

As Latter-day Saints we often emphasize our distinctive belief in God's corporeal nature (how God is like man), but we must never forget that the Being we worship is also an exalted, glorified Being whose body, unlike man's, is divine. Moses wrote that "the sight of the glory of the Lord was like devouring fire on the top of the mount in the eyes of the children of Israel" (Exodus 24:17). Similarly, in speaking through Isaiah, Jehovah asked, "Who among us shall dwell with the devouring fire? who among us shall dwell with everlasting burnings?" (Isaiah 33:14). In his vision of the celestial kingdom, received in January 1836, Joseph Smith explained, "I saw the transcendent beauty of the gate through which the heirs of that [celestial] kingdom will enter, which was like unto circling flames of fire; also the blazing throne of God, whereon was seated the Father and the Son" (D&C 137:2–3). In his King Follett sermon, the Prophet observed, "How consoling to the mourners when they are called to part with a husband, wife, father, mother, child, or dear relative, to know that, although the earthly tabernacle is laid down and dissolved, they shall rise again to dwell in everlasting burnings in immortal glory."[9] In short, the First Vision established indelibly in the mind of young Joseph what he came to know even more forcefully as the years passed: "God Almighty Himself dwells in eternal fire; flesh and blood cannot go there, for all corruption is devoured by the fire. 'Our God is a consuming fire.'"[10]

Redemption through Jesus Christ

Joseph Smith also learned firsthand of the life beyond mortality and of the immortality of the soul. He became, early in his ministry, a witness of the Resurrection, for before him stood the resurrected Lord Jesus, attesting that indeed life did continue beyond the grave and that immortal life does come through the inseparable union of body and spirit. In fact, according to the earliest account of the First Vision (1832), the testimony of Jesus and the efficacy of his redeeming labor were among the first things Joseph was taught. "I cried unto the Lord for mercy," he stated, "for there was none else to whom I could go and obtain mercy. And the Lord heard my cry in the wilderness, and while [I was] in the attitude of calling upon the Lord . . . a pillar of light above the brightness of the sun at noon day came down from above and rested upon me, and I was filled with the Spirit of God. And the Lord opened the heavens upon me and I saw the Lord and he spake unto me, saying, 'Joseph, my son, thy sins are forgiven thee; go thy way; walk in my statutes; and keep my commandments. Behold, I am the Lord of glory. I was crucified for the world, that all those who believe on my name may have eternal life. . . .' My soul was filled with love, and for many days I could rejoice with great joy and the Lord was with me."[11]

The Nature of the Father and the Son

Brother Joseph learned that the Father and the Son were separate and distinct personages, separate Gods, and thus that creeds concerning a triune deity were incorrect. For example, although

Unitarians believed that the first and second members of the Godhead were distinct beings, most Christians subscribed to the doctrine of the Trinity. Only eleven days before his death, the Prophet stated, "I have always declared God to be a distinct personage, Jesus Christ a separate and distinct personage from God the Father, and that the Holy Ghost was a distinct personage and a Spirit: and these three constitute three distinct personages and three Gods."[12]

We are uncertain what the young prophet learned at the time of the First Vision relative to the corporeality, or physical nature, of God the Father. Joseph certainly may have been taught or recognized that God has a physical body, but we do not have record of his saying so. We do, however, have the following from his translation of Genesis (November-December 1830), now Moses 6: "In the day that God created man, in the likeness of God made he him; *in the image of his own body, male and female, created he them,* and blessed them" (Moses 6:8–9; emphasis added). In 1836 Reverend Truman Coe, a Presbyterian minister who had lived among the Saints in Kirtland for four years, wrote in a local newspaper of some of the beliefs of the Latter-day Saints. "They believe that the true God is a material being," he explained, "composed of body and parts; and that when the Creator formed Adam in his own image, he made him about the size and shape of God himself."[13] William Clayton recorded that on 5 January 1841 the Prophet Joseph declared: "That which is without body and parts is nothing. There is no other God in heaven but that God who has flesh and bones."[14] On 9 March 1841 he spoke of the ministries of Jesus as the Mediator and the Holy Ghost as the Witness or Testator. He then stated that "the Son had a tabernacle and so had the Father."[15] Finally, on 2 April 1843 in Ramus, Illinois, Joseph the Prophet delivered instructions on this matter that are the basis for Doctrine and Covenants 130:22–23: "The Father has a body of flesh and bones as tangible as man's; the Son also; but the Holy Ghost . . . is a personage of Spirit."

Order in the Kingdom of God

The young Joseph noted that "just at this moment of great alarm, I saw a pillar of light exactly over my head, above the brightness of the sun, which descended gradually until it fell upon me.

"It no sooner appeared than I found myself delivered from the enemy which held me bound. When the light rested upon me I saw two Personages, whose brightness and glory defy all description, standing above me in the air. One of them spake unto me, calling me by name and said, pointing to the other—This is my Beloved Son. Hear Him!" (Joseph Smith–History 1:16–17).

There is order in the kingdom of God. The Father introduces the Son, who then speaks to the Prophet. The King James Version of John 1:18 states, "No man hath seen God at any time: the only begotten Son, which is in the bosom of the Father, he hath declared him." Under inspiration, Joseph the Seer altered that verse as follows: "And no man hath seen God at any time, *except he hath borne record of the Son;* for except it is through him no man can be saved" (JST John 1:19; emphasis added; see also JST Psalm 14:1; JST 1 John 4:12).

"We have a wonderful illustration," President Joseph Fielding Smith taught, "of how revelation comes through Christ presented to us in the Vision given to the Prophet Joseph Smith. The Father and the Son appeared unto him, but it was not the Father who answered his question! The Father introduced Joseph to his Son, and it was the Son who answered the important question and gave the instruction.

"Had Joseph Smith come home from the grove and declared that the Father and the Son appeared to him and that the Father spoke to him and answered his question while the Son stood silently by, then we could have accepted the story as a fraud. Joseph Smith was too young and inexperienced to know this at the time, but he made no mistake, and his story was in perfect harmony with divine truth, with the divine law that Christ is the Mediator between God and man."[16]

The Fulness of the Gospel Was Not on the Earth

Joseph learned that the Church of Jesus Christ, as established by the Savior himself and his apostles in the meridian of time, had not continued during the centuries in its pristine purity. He was therefore instructed to join none of the churches in the area. "They told me that all religious denominations were believing in incorrect doctrines, and that none of them was acknowledged of God as his church and kingdom. And I was expressly commanded to 'go not after them,' at the same time receiving a promise that the fulness of the gospel should at some future time be made known unto me."[17]

JOSEPH SMITH AND THE REVELATION OF CHRIST

Joseph Smith's introduction to Jesus Christ came in the Sacred Grove in the spring of 1820. Reaffirmed in that monumental theophany was the fundamental Christian teaching that Jesus of Nazareth lived, died, was buried, and rose from the tomb in glorious immortality. In the midst of the light that shone above the brightness of the sun stood the resurrected Lord Jesus in company with his Father, the Almighty Elohim. Joseph Smith knew from the time of the First Vision that death was not the end, that life continues after our physical demise, that another realm of existence— a postmortal sphere—does in fact exist. Through open vision, by visitations, and by voice Joseph Smith came to know his Lord as few men have ever known him. The revelations that came through Joseph Smith made the latter-day seer acquainted with the mind and voice and will of the Master. Joseph came to know firsthand how to commune with Jehovah.

Like Jesus, the Prophet Joseph Smith was called upon to endure a life of loneliness. It was a life characterized by persecution and suspicion, an isolated existence known only to those who walk in the glorious light of the noonday sun, who know with an absolute certainty and yet must minister among others who seem to walk and talk in the fading rays of dusk, those who struggle with faith, those who doubt, and even those who dare not believe. The farm boy who grew to become a prophet could bear a personal witness of his divine Redeemer, for Joseph was also, to some degree at least, a man of sorrows and acquainted with grief (see Isaiah 53:3), one who knew directly the costs of Christian discipleship. "God is my friend," he wrote to his wife Emma at a difficult time. "In him I shall find comfort. I have given my life into his hands. I am prepared to go at his call. I desire to be with Christ. I count not my life dear to me, only to do his will."[18] Such expressions enable us to discern the soul of Joseph Smith, to discover the underlying secret of his success—his humility. He knew, and he wanted all others to know, that he walked in the shadow of the Almighty. He was the prophet of the Almighty; God knew it, and he knew it.

Anciently, when Aaron and Miriam allowed themselves to be embroiled in a critical spirit toward their brother Moses, Jehovah declared: "If there be a prophet among you, I the Lord will make myself known unto him in a vision, and will speak unto him in a dream.

"My servant Moses is not so, who is faithful in all mine house.

"With him will I speak mouth to mouth, even apparently, and not in dark speeches; and the similitude of the Lord shall he behold: wherefore then were ye not afraid to speak against my servant Moses?" (Numbers 12:6–8).

We learn from this exchange an important principle: there are prophets, and then there are prophets. The apostle Paul explained that "the spirits of the prophets are subject to the prophets" (1 Corinthians 14:32). There is an order, a hierarchy, even among those called as oracles and mouthpieces of the Almighty.

Jesus Christ is the presiding officer in the kingdom of God, the Great High Priest of our profession (Hebrews 3:1). The Prophet Joseph explained that after Christ in the government of the kingdom of God comes Adam and then Noah.[19] "You start out with the Lord Jesus," Elder Bruce R. McConkie observed, "and then you have Adam and Noah. Thereafter come the dispensation heads. Then you step down, appreciably, and come to prophets and apostles, to the elders of Israel, and to wise and good and sagacious men who have the spirit of light and understanding."[20]

Joseph Smith, like Adam, Enoch, Noah, Abraham, Moses, Jesus, and others, stands as a dispensation head. The dispensation head becomes the means by which the knowledge and power of God are channeled to men and women on earth. He becomes the means by which the gospel of Jesus Christ—God's plan of salvation—is revealed anew, the means by which divine transforming powers, including saving covenants and ordinances, are extended to people during an age of time we call a dispensation.

The dispensation head stands as the preeminent prophetic revealer and witness of Christ; he knows firsthand because of what he has seen and heard and felt and experienced. Because of his central place in the plan, because it is by means of the power of his testimony that men and women come to know the Lord and bask in the light of the Spirit, the calling and position of the dispensation head thus becomes something about which his followers feel to bear witness. Indeed, and appropriately so, men and women of a particular dispensation who stand to express the witness that burns in their bosoms, find themselves bearing testimony of Christ and of the dispensation head—the revealer of Christ—in almost the same breath. This is just as it should be.

Elder McConkie thus pointed out: "Every prophet is a witness of Christ; every dispensation head is a revealer of Christ for his day; and every other prophet or apostle who comes is a reflection and an echo and an exponent of the dispensation head. All such come to echo to the world and to expound and unfold what God has revealed to the man who was appointed for that era to give his eternal word to the world. Such is the dispensation concept."[21]

Thus the Savior declared to Joseph Smith: "This generation shall have my word through you" (D&C 5:10). Thomas B. Marsh was instructed to "declare glad tidings of great joy unto this generation." And what did that entail? Was Brother Marsh to restate the Sermon on the Mount? Was he to reemphasize the poignant message in our Savior's Bread of Life Sermon? Was he to discuss at length the Lord's teachings at the Last Supper? Of course he was to prize and treasure the message of the Bible, but his witness and his declaration were to be current. "You shall declare the things which have been revealed to my servant, Joseph Smith, Jun." (D&C 31:4).

If the full knowledge and power of God are to be had in this final dispensation, they will be had through the work set in motion and the truths that flowed and the authorities transmitted by and through Joseph Smith, or they will be had not at all. To bear witness that Joseph Smith is a prophet is to testify that (1) he was a revealer of truth, divine truth, and more particularly, the truths concerning Jesus Christ; and (2) that he was a legal administrator, a conduit by which the keys of the kingdom of God have been conferred once again upon men.

Occasionally we hear people complain that they hear too few testimonies of Christ and too many of Joseph Smith. To be sure, we worship the Father in the name of the Son, Christ our Lord is the way to the Father (John 14:6), and his is the only name under heaven whereby man can be saved (Acts 4:12; Mosiah 3:17). And yet, we have seen that the dispensation head is the preeminent prophetic revealer of Christ. Thus to bear witness of Joseph Smith is to bear witness of Jesus Christ who sent him, just as to bear witness of Christ is to bear witness of the Father who sent him. Jesus told his disciples that "he that despiseth you despiseth me; and he that despiseth me despiseth him that sent me" (Luke 10:16; compare D&C 1:38; 84:36; 112:20).

President Joseph F. Smith, nephew of the Prophet, declared: "I believe in the divinity of Jesus Christ, because more than ever I have come nearer the possession of the actual knowledge that Jesus is the Christ, the Son of the living God, through the testimony of Joseph Smith . . . that he saw Him, that he heard Him, that he received instructions from Him, that he obeyed those instructions, and that he today stands before the world as the last great, actual, living, witness of the divinity of Christ's mission and [Christ's] power to redeem man. . . . Thank God for Joseph Smith."[22]

CONCLUSION

Joseph Smith's First Vision is fundamental to the faith of Latter-day Saints. It represents the beginning of the re-revelation of God to man in this final dispensation. President George Q. Cannon, who loved the Prophet Joseph Smith with all his heart, summarized beautifully the entire experience as follows:

"It was one morning in early springtime of the year 1820, that Joseph felt the earnest prompting and adopted the holy resolve. He walked into the depths of a wood, which stood near his home, and sought a little glade. There, in trembling humility, but with a faith which thrilled his soul—alone, unseen of man, he fell upon his knees and lifted his voice in prayer to God. While he was calling upon the Almighty, a subtle and malignant power seized him and stilled his utterance. Deep darkness enveloped him; he felt that he was in the grasp of Satan, and that the destroyer was exerting all the power of hell to drag him to sudden destruction. In his agony he called anew upon the Lord for deliverance; and at the moment when he seemed to be sinking under the power of the evil one, the deep gloom was rolled away and he saw a brilliant light. A pillar of celestial fire, far more glorious than the brightness of the noonday sun, appeared directly above him. The defeated power fled with the darkness; and Joseph's spirit was free to worship and marvel at his deliverance. Gradually the light descended until it rested upon him; and he saw, standing above him in the air, enveloped in the pure radiance of the fiery pillar, two Personages of incomparable beauty, alike in form and feature, and clad alike in snowy raiment. Sublime, dazzling, they filled his soul with awe. At length, one, calling Joseph by name, stretched His shining arm towards the other, and said:

"'This is my beloved Son: Hear Him!'

"As soon as Joseph could regain possession of himself, to which he was encouraged by the benign and comforting look of the Son, and by the heavenly bliss which pervaded his own soul, he found words to ask, which of all the multitude of churches upon the face of the globe had the gospel of Christ; for up to this time it had never entered his mind to doubt that the true church of the Lamb, pure and undefiled, had an existence somewhere among men. But the answer came that no one of the creeds of earth was pure, and that Joseph must unite himself with none of them. Said the glorious Being:

"'They draw near me with their lips, but their hearts are far from me; they teach for doctrine the commandments of men, having a form of godliness, but they deny the power thereof.'

"Even in the transport of his vision, Joseph felt amazed at the instruction. But the Heavenly Personages continued to commune with him, and repeated their command that he should not ally himself with any of the man-made sects. Then they and their enclosing pillar of light passed from his gaze, and he was left to look into the immensity of space.

"The boy's faith in the promises of God had now deepened into knowledge. He had been assailed by the power of evil, until it seemed he must succumb—that the limit of human endurance was passed. And in that instant of deepest despair, he had been suddenly transported into the blaze of celestial light. He had seen with his own eyes the Father and the Son, with his own ears he had heard their eternal voices. Over this untaught youth at least, the heavens were no longer as brass. He had emerged from the maze of doubt and uncertainty in which he had so long groped, and had received positive assurances on the matter nearest his heart from Him, whom to know was anciently declared to be life eternal."[23]

Elder Orson Pratt testified: "Now here was a certainty; here was something that he saw and heard; here were personages capable of instructing him, and of telling him which was the true religion. How different this was from going to an uninspired man. . . . One minute's instruction from personages clothed with the glory of God coming down from the eternal worlds is worth more than all the volumes that ever were written by uninspired men."[24]

"Nothing short of this total vision to Joseph could have served the purpose to clear away the mists of the centuries," President Spencer W. Kimball attested. "Merely an impression, a hidden voice, a dream could [not] have dispelled the old vagaries and misconceptions. . . . The God of all these worlds and the Son of God, the Redeemer, our Savior, in person attended this boy. He saw the living God. He saw the living Christ."[25]

President Gordon B. Hinckley rejoiced: "To me it is a significant and marvelous thing that in establishing and opening this dispensation our Father did so with a revelation of himself and of his

Son Jesus Christ, as if to say to all the world that he was weary of the attempts of men, earnest though these attempts might have been, to define and describe him. . . . The experience of Joseph Smith in a few moments in the grove on a spring day in 1820, brought more light and knowledge and understanding of the personality and reality and substance of God and his Beloved Son than men had arrived at during centuries of speculation."[26]

On a more personal note, I have always believed there is a God. My earliest memories of childhood contain familiar words spoken beside my bed each night: "Now I lay me down to sleep. . . ." It felt right to say my prayers, and I sincerely believed that I was being heard by someone far wiser, greater, and more powerful and loving than anyone here on earth. Further, having grown up in the Southern States, with most of my friends being Baptists, Methodists, and Roman Catholics, I sang with them songs having lines such as "Jesus loves me, this I know, for the Bible tells me so" and "Jesus wants me for a sunbeam" with gusto and feeling. It seems that I have always believed in the living reality of Jesus Christ as the Savior and Redeemer of humankind.

My grandfather joined The Church of Jesus Christ of Latter-day Saints in the 1930s near New Orleans, Louisiana. He had been brought up as a Roman Catholic, and when he left the faith of his fathers, he was, essentially, asked to leave his home. Later he and my grandmother raised their four sons as Latter-day Saints. At the time I was born, my father and mother were not active church attenders, but in time they felt the need to raise their children in the Church. I recall being asked to speak in church when I was about nine years old. My father did not feel at that stage of his spiritual development that he was in a position to help me much, and so my Uncle Joseph essentially wrote my talk for me. I memorized it. It was a very simple recitation of Joseph Smith's First Vision—the story of how young Joseph wrestled in 1820 with which church to join, how he encountered varying and conflicting views on religious questions, and how he chose to follow the scriptural admonition to ask God for wisdom (James 1:5).

It has now been more than fifty years since I looked out at that rather frightening congregation, delivered those memorized words (in a talk that couldn't have lasted more than a very few minutes), and then sat down with a feeling of overwhelming relief. I also remember something else about that occasion—namely, how I felt at the time I spoke about God the Father and his Son Jesus Christ appearing to a fourteen-year-old boy in upstate New York. Although I was nervous and fidgety behind the pulpit, I began on that occasion to feel the stirrings of testimony, the beginnings of a spiritual witness, that what I was speaking about was true and that it had actually happened. The relief I felt was not simply the flood of emotion associated with having completed a daunting task but also the quiet, poignant assurance that I had spoken the truth. I knew something when I sat down that I had not known before I stood up to speak.

I have had thousands of confirming witnesses of the truthfulness of Joseph Smith's claim since I stood and addressed those people in the old Hiawatha Street Chapel in Baton Rouge, Louisiana. And it has been my honor and privilege to bear testimony of that singular event throughout the United States and in several foreign countries. Over the past several years, I have returned often to Palmyra, New York, to the Sacred Grove. Every time I have come away with an overwhelming sense of responsibility to bear testimony of foundational truths, especially Joseph Smith's First Vision.

I know that Jesus is the Christ, the Son of the Living God, in the same way that Peter knew it anciently—by the power of revelation from God our Father (Matthew 16:13–17). By that same Spirit I know that Joseph Smith saw the Father and the Son in the spring of 1820 in the grove. That witness is central to all I believe and feel and do as a Latter-day Saint. Times change, people come and go, and circumstances and challenges change, but for me the First Vision is a constant, a foundation stone, a pillar of my personal religious life.

CHAPTER TWO

SETTING THE KEYSTONE

On Sunday, 28 November 1841, the Prophet Joseph Smith met with the Nauvoo city council and members of the Quorum of the Twelve in the home of President Brigham Young. History records that he conversed "with them upon a variety of subjects."[1] In the Youngs' residence, Joseph Smith made one of the most axiomatic and memorable statements in Mormon literature, one that has elicited warmth, commitment, curiosity, disdain, and even persecution. "I told the brethren," he said, "that the Book of Mormon was the most correct of any book on earth, and the keystone of our religion, and a man would get nearer to God by abiding by its precepts, than by any other book."[2]

Let us consider the possible meaning and implications of the various parts of this bold declaration about this extrabiblical document—the nature of its correctness, how it is the keystone, the ways it contributes to our religion, the poignancy of its precepts, its power to draw us to God, and, finally, its prophetic destiny as a book of holy scripture.

THE MOST CORRECT BOOK

How is the Book of Mormon the most correct of any book? In Joseph Smith's day the word *correct* was understood to mean "set right, made straight," "conformable to truth, rectitude or propriety, or conformable to a just standard; not faulty; free from error." Likewise, to correct something was "to amend" or to "bring back or attempt to bring back to propriety," to "obviate or remove whatever is wrong" or to "counteract whatever is injurious."[3] In our day we say that something is correct if it is "free from error; accurate; in accordance with fact, truth, or reason."[4] In all those senses, then, the Book of Mormon was given to us to set things straight, to make things right, to bring our thinking into conformity with truth (with things as they really are; see Jacob 4:13; compare D&C 93:24), to bring back or restore to propriety, and to counteract ideas or teachings or practices that are harmful.

Nephi beheld in vision that after plain and precious truths had been taken away or kept back from the Bible and the gospel in general, the Lord would bring forth the Book of Mormon and "other books": "And in them shall be written my gospel, saith the Lamb, and my rock and my salvation . . . unto the convincing of the Gentiles and the remnant of the seed of thy brethren, and also the Jews . . . that the records of the prophets and of the twelve apostles of the Lamb are true." In short, the Restoration scriptures "shall establish the truth of the first" and "shall make known the plain and precious things which have been taken away from them [the Bible]; and shall make known to all kindreds, tongues, and people, that the Lamb of God is the Son of the Eternal Father, and the Savior of the world; and that all men must come unto him, or they cannot be saved" (1 Nephi 13:36, 39–40).

We are acquainted with Ezekiel's prophecy that the stick of Judah and the stick of Ephraim would become one in the hand of

Jehovah, a poignant symbol of the ultimate gathering and uniting of the two formerly estranged nations (Ezekiel 37:15–22). We learn the following from a prophecy of Joseph who was sold into Egypt these words of Jehovah, words later excerpted by Lehi in counseling his young son Joseph: "The fruit of thy loins shall write [the Book of Mormon]; and the fruit of the loins of Judah shall write [the Bible]; and that which shall be written by the fruit of thy loins, and also that which shall be written by the fruit of the loins of Judah, shall grow together." And why would they grow together? For the purpose of "the confounding of false doctrines and laying down of contentions, and establishing peace among the fruit of thy loins, and bringing them to the knowledge of their fathers in the latter days, and also to the knowledge of my covenants, saith the Lord" (2 Nephi 3:12; see also JST Genesis 50).

I believe the Bible to be the word of God and a marvelous witness of the Almighty's love and tender mercies; of his eagerness to bless and prosper those who put their trust in him; and of the central, saving significance of the Messiah, the Christ, the Anointed One. I love the Bible, especially the New Testament, for the manner in which it beckons me to submit to the divine will and surrender my hopes and dreams to him who can do far more with my life than I can. I believe with all my heart that the Bible is meant to be read and pondered and memorized and applied by the Latter-day Saints and by all of God's children; it contains the fulness of the gospel of the Lamb. Having affirmed my love for the Bible, I hasten to add (as the Book of Mormon teaches) that I do not believe it has come down to us in its pristine purity, as it was written by the original writers.[5] This perspective does not, however, weaken my faith in its essential and central messages. Rather, it makes me more grateful for the scriptures of the Restoration that strive to prove "to the world that the holy scriptures are true" (D&C 20:11).

Why is it important to know the truthfulness of the Bible? A growing proportion of people in our world have begun to discount, belittle, or deny the elements of holy scripture that make them matter—divine intervention, miracles, and predictive prophecy. In fact, the "quest for the historical Jesus" has retrogressed to the point of an outright rejection of our Lord's divinity and his bodily resurrection from the dead—and this on the part of people who still desire to be known as Christians. In 1966 Elder Gordon B. Hinckley said: "Modern theologians strip [Jesus] of his divinity and then wonder why men do not worship him. These clever scholars have taken from Jesus the mantle of godhood and have left only a man. They have tried to accommodate him to their own narrow thinking. They have robbed him of his divine Sonship and taken from the world its rightful King."[6]

President Harold B. Lee explained to a group of students at Utah State University: "Fifty years ago or more," he said, "there were the unmistakable evidences that there was coming into the religious world actually a question about the Bible and about the divine calling of the Master himself. Now, fifty years later [1971], our greatest responsibility and anxiety is to defend the divine mission of our Lord and Master, Jesus Christ, for all about us, even among those who claim to be professors of the Christian faith, are those not willing to stand squarely in defense of the great truth that our Lord and Master, Jesus Christ, was indeed the Son of God."[7]

From my perspective, the Book of Mormon is the most correct of any book on earth because of the undiluted and penetrating message it presents—the way it establishes in no uncertain terms that "there is a God in heaven, who is infinite and eternal, from everlasting to everlasting the same unchangeable God, the framer of heaven and earth, and all things which are in them" (D&C 20:17); the way it highlights the nature of fallen humanity; the way it focuses repeatedly upon man's utter inability to forgive or cleanse or resurrect or save himself; the way it places Jesus Christ on center stage and testifies of the infinite and eternal scope of his atoning sacrifice. In the Book of Mormon, Christ is the Lord God Omnipotent who saves "not only those who believed after he came in the meridian of time, in the flesh, but all those from the beginning, even as many as were before he came, who believed in the words of the holy prophets, . . . as well as those who should come after" (D&C 20:26–27). For me the Book of Mormon is the most correct book on earth because it teaches us who God is, what the Godhead is, how they are infinitely more one that they are separate, and how the love and unity between the Father, Son, and Holy Ghost is of such magnitude that the Nephite record speaks of them several times simply as "one God, infinite and eternal, without end" (D&C 20:28; compare 2 Nephi 31:21; Alma 11:44; 3 Nephi 9:15; 11:27, 36; 28:10; Mormon 7:7). I believe the Book of Mormon is the most correct book because it presents with consistent clarity the delicate balance between the mercy and grace of our Lord and God and the works of righteousness that must always characterize and identify true disciples of the Master (2 Nephi 2:2–8; 25:23; 31:19; Alma 22:14; Helaman 14:13; Moroni 6:4).

I believe the Book of Mormon to be the most correct scriptural book because it assists us to span the Testaments and consequently span the chasm that many feel exists between the God of the Old and the God of the New. "I make my own heartfelt declaration of God, our Eternal Father," Elder Jeffrey R. Holland stated, "because some in the contemporary world suffer from a distressing misconception of Him. Among these there is a tendency to feel distant from the Father, even estranged from Him, if they believe in Him at all. And if they do believe, many moderns say they might feel comfortable in the arms of Jesus, but they are uneasy contemplating the stern encounter of God."

Elder Holland observed further that "one of the remarkable contributions of the Book of Mormon is its seamless, perfectly consistent view of divinity throughout that majestic book. Here there is no Malachi-to-Matthew gap, no pause while we shift theological gears, no misreading the God who is urgently, lovingly, faithfully at work on every page of that record from its Old Testament beginning to its New Testament end. Yes, in an effort to give the world back its Bible and a correct view of Deity with it, what we have in the Book of Mormon is a uniform view of God in all His glory and goodness, all His richness and complexity—including and especially as again demonstrated through a personal appearance of His Only Begotten Son, Jesus Christ."

Finally, Elder Holland pointed out that "Jesus did not come to improve God's view of man nearly so much as He came to improve men's view of God and to plead with them to love their Heavenly Father as He has always and will always love them. The plan of God, the power of God, the holiness of God, yes, even the anger and the judgment of God they had occasion to understand. But the love of God, the profound depth of His devotion to His children, they still did not fully know—until Christ came."[8]

Our belief as Latter-day Saints in the supreme correctness of this other Testament of Jesus Christ is not a denial of the Bible nor is it a statement that the former is wholly correct and the latter is wholly incorrect. Moroni himself acknowledged that the Book of Mormon may contain human error (Title Page; Mormon 8:17). The very fact that we study and teach the Bible in our own homes and in the meetings of the Church, general and local, is a statement that we treasure its content and seek to conform our lives to its timeless counsel.

THE KEYSTONE

The Prophet Joseph characterized the Book of Mormon as "the keystone of our religion." Recently Elder Jeffrey R. Holland described the function of a keystone as follows: "A keystone is positioned at the uppermost center of an arch in such a way as to hold all the other stones in place. That key piece, if removed, will bring all of the other blocks crashing down with it."[9]

What does this mean in regard to the Book of Mormon? President Ezra Taft Benson explained that the Book of Mormon "is the keystone in our witness of Christ . . . the keystone of our doctrine" and "the keystone of [our] testimony."[10] He taught: "The Book of Mormon is the keystone in our witness of Jesus Christ, who is Himself the cornerstone of everything we do. It bears witness of His reality with power and clarity. Unlike the Bible, which passed through generations of copyists, translators, and corrupt religionists who tampered with the text, the Book of Mormon came from writer to reader in just one inspired step of translation. Therefore, its testimony of the Master is clear, undiluted, and full of power. But it does even more. Much of the Christian world today rejects the divinity of the Savior. They question His miraculous birth, His perfect life, and the reality of His glorious resurrection. The Book of Mormon teaches in plain and unmistakable terms about the truth of all of those. It also provides the most complete explanation of the doctrine of the Atonement."[11]

As to the Book of Mormon being the keystone of our doctrine, President Benson reminded us that it contains what the scriptures call "the fulness of the gospel" (D&C 20:9; 27:5; 42:12; 135:3). It is not the case that this scriptural record contains the fulness of Latter-day Saint doctrines, for there is no mention in the Book of Mormon of such matters as eternal marriage, three degrees of glory, or the corporeality of God. The Book of Mormon contains the fulness of the gospel in the sense that it declares and elevates the core truth of salvation in Christ—including the good news, or glad tidings, of the Atonement (3 Nephi 27:13–14), as well as the means by which we incorporate the Atonement into our lives through the first principles and ordinances (2 Nephi 31; 3 Nephi 27:15–21). In short, "in the Book of Mormon we will find the fulness of those doctrines required for our salvation. And they are taught plainly and simply so that even children can learn the ways of salvation and exaltation. The Book of Mormon offers so much that broadens our understandings of the doctrines of salvation. Without it, much of what is taught in other scriptures would not be nearly so plain and precious."[12]

Simply stated, if either the story of the origins or the message of the book itself is false, the whole religious system that is built upon and flows from the book, including our individual and collective testimonies of the Restoration, are false, misleading, and thus spiritually destructive. "The enemies of the Church understand this clearly," President Benson noted. "This is why they go to such great lengths to try to disprove the Book of Mormon, for if it can be discredited, the Prophet Joseph Smith goes with it. So does our claim to priesthood keys, and revelation, and the restored Church."[13]

Elder Jeffrey R. Holland likewise has written: "To consider that everything of saving significance in the Church stands or falls on the truthfulness of the Book of Mormon and, by implication, the Prophet Joseph Smith's account of how it came forth is as sobering as it is true. It is a 'sudden-death' proposition. Either the Book of Mormon is what the Prophet Joseph said it is, or this church and its founder are false, a deception from the first instance onward.

"Not everything in life is so black and white," Elder Holland observed, "but the authenticity of the Book of Mormon and its keystone role in our religion seem to be exactly that."[14] If Moroni did not truly appear to the seventeen-year-old Joseph Smith Jr. on 21 September 1823; if Joseph and the Witnesses did not heft and handle actual, tangible, physical, metal plates with the appearance of gold; if Joseph and his scribes did not translate the Book of

Mormon by the gift and power of God through the Urim and Thummim, Joseph "would not be entitled to the reputation of New England folk hero or well-meaning young man or writer of remarkable fiction. No, nor would he be entitled to be considered a great teacher, a quintessential American religious leader, or the creator of great devotional literature. If he had lied about the coming forth of the Book of Mormon, he would certainly be none of these.

"I am suggesting," Elder Holland stated soberly, "that one has to take something of a do-or-die stand regarding the restoration of the gospel of Jesus Christ and the divine origins of the Book of Mormon. Reason and righteousness require it. Joseph Smith must be accepted either as a prophet of God or else as a charlatan of the first order, but no one should tolerate any ludicrous, even laughable middle ground about the wonderful contours of a young boy's imagination or his remarkable facility for turning a literary phrase. That is an unacceptable position to take—morally, literarily, historically, or theologically."[15]

Obedience to Its Precepts

A *precept* is a command, a mandate, an order pertaining to proper behavior.[16] It is "a general instruction or rule for action, a maxim; *esp.* an injunction (freq. a divine command) regarding moral conduct."[17] Joseph Smith's statement avers that a person will draw nearer to God by abiding by the precepts of the Book of Mormon than by any other book. It would seem that attending scrupulously to the ever-present "and thus we see" or "and thus we can plainly discern" statements and then abiding by them would be a significant part of our obedience. These appear to be the various prophets' means of stating to the reader: "In case you didn't get the point of this story or that episode or this tragedy or that happy ending, let me make it clear by formulating it into a maxim or a memorable saying. It is something that should not be ignored or forgotten."

Precepts could obviously take the form of "thou shalts" and "thou shalt nots," warnings against violating the Ten Commandments or committing such sins as pride, greed, immorality, arrogance, indifference, profanity, rebellion, and a failure to remember. On the positive side are precepts that invite us to give mind and heart to transcendent truths, liberating and lasting lessons.

Consider the following sublime insights from the Book of Mormon:

"The tender mercies of the Lord are over all those he hath chosen, because of their faith, to make them mighty even unto the power of deliverance" (1 Nephi 1:20).

"And they did murmur because they knew not the mind of that God who had created them" (1 Nephi 2:12).

"I will go and do the things which the Lord hath commanded, for I know that the Lord giveth no commandments unto the children of men, save he shall prepare a way for them that they may accomplish the thing which he commandeth them" (1 Nephi 3:7).

"All mankind [are] in a lost and in a fallen state, and ever [will] be save they [shall] rely on this Redeemer" (1 Nephi 10:6).

"[God] is the same yesterday, today, and forever; and the way is prepared for all men from the foundation of the world, if it so be that they repent and come unto him. For he that diligently seeketh shall find; and the mysteries of God shall be unfolded unto them, by the power of the Holy Ghost, as well in these times as in times of old . . . ; wherefore, the course of the Lord is one eternal round" (1 Nephi 10:18–19).

"By small means the Lord can bring about great things" (1 Nephi 16:29).

"Behold, the Lord esteemeth all flesh in one; he that is righteous is favored of God" (1 Nephi 17:35).

"I did liken all scriptures unto us, that it might be for our profit and learning" (1 Nephi 19:23).

"Wherefore, I know that thou art redeemed, because of the righteousness of thy Redeemer" (2 Nephi 2:3).

"Adam fell that men might be; and men are, that they might have joy. And the Messiah cometh in the fulness of time, that he may redeem the children of men from the fall. And because that they are redeemed from the fall they have become free forever, knowing good from evil; to act for themselves and not to be acted upon" (2 Nephi 2:25–26).

"O Lord, I have trusted in thee, and I will trust in thee forever. I will not put my trust in the arm of flesh" (2 Nephi 4:34).

"O how great the holiness of our God! For he knoweth all things, and there is not anything save he knows it" (2 Nephi 9:20).

"O that cunning plan of the evil one! O the vainness, and the frailties, and the foolishness of men! When they are learned they think they are wise, and they hearken not unto the counsel of God, for they set it aside, supposing they know of themselves, wherefore, their wisdom is foolishness and it profiteth them not. And they shall perish. But to be learned is good if they hearken unto the counsels of God" (2 Nephi 9:28–29).

"Remember, to be carnally minded is death, and to be spiritually minded is life eternal" (2 Nephi 9:39).

"Wherefore, my beloved brethren, reconcile yourselves to the will of God, and not to the will of the devil and the flesh; and remember, after ye are reconciled unto God, that it is only in and through the grace of God that ye are saved" (2 Nephi 10:24).

"For we labor diligently to write, to persuade our children, and also our brethren, to believe in Christ, and to be reconciled to God; for we know that it is by grace that we are saved, after all we can do" (2 Nephi 25:23).

"And we talk of Christ, we rejoice in Christ, we preach of

Christ, we prophesy of Christ, and we write according to our prophecies, that our children may know to what source they may look for a remission of their sins" (2 Nephi 25:26).

"The Lord God worketh not in darkness. He doeth not anything save it be for the benefit of the world; for he loveth the world, even that he layeth down his own life that he may draw all men unto him. Wherefore, he commandeth none that they shall not partake of his salvation" (2 Nephi 26:23–24).

"Believe in God; believe that he is, and that he created all things, both in heaven and in earth; believe that he has all wisdom, and all power, both in heaven and in earth; believe that man doth not comprehend all the things which the Lord can comprehend" (Mosiah 4:9).

"O how marvelous are the works of the Lord, and how long doth he suffer with his people; yea, and how blind and impenetrable are the understandings of the children of men; for they will not seek wisdom, neither do they desire that she should rule over them" (Mosiah 8:20).

This sampling of passages demonstrates the wisdom and power and learning of heaven that flow from the pages of the Book of Mormon. And how do we sum it all up? Moroni, interjecting his thoughts and the yearnings of his soul into his abridgment of the Jaredite record, wrote: "And now, I would commend you to seek this Jesus of whom the prophets and apostles have written, that the grace of God the Father, and also the Lord Jesus Christ, and the Holy Ghost, which beareth record of them, may be and abide in you forever. Amen" (Ether 12:41).

Passages such as these demand a reasonable explanation. Where did they come from? Who wrote them? Was Joseph Smith really that bright, that articulate, that eloquent, that polished in his presentation of sacred truths? Someone commented to me recently that it takes too much faith to be an atheist! I agree wholeheartedly.

And I am persuaded—setting aside the living witness within my mind and heart of the truthfulness of the Book of Mormon—that it is much easier to believe in angels and golden plates and seer stones than to accept some of the ridiculous explanations that critics of the book offer. "If Joseph Smith did not translate the Book of Mormon as a work of ancient origin," Elder Jeffrey R. Holland has written, "then I would move heaven and earth to meet the 'real' nineteenth-century author. After one hundred and fifty years, no one can come up with a credible alternative candidate, but if the book were false, surely there must be someone willing to step forward—if no one else, at least the descendants of the 'real' author—claiming credit for such a remarkable document and all that has transpired in its wake. After all, a writer that can move millions can make millions. Shouldn't someone have come forth then or now to cashier the whole phenomenon?"

The fact is, Elder Holland concluded, "there is no other clandestine 'author,' no elusive ghostwriter still waiting in the wings after a century and a half for the chance to stride forward and startle the religious world. Indeed, that any writer—Joseph Smith or anyone else—could create the Book of Mormon out of whole cloth would be an infinitely greater miracle than that young Joseph translated it from an ancient record 'by the gift and power of God.'"[18]

An acquaintance of mine from another faith—a prominent pastor, teacher, and writer—explained to me in a letter that he had finally decided that the explanations offered by anti-Mormon critics for the origin of the Book of Mormon were oversimplistic and downright silly; the book was too complex to explain it away through some connection with Solomon Spaulding, Ethan Smith, or Sidney Rigdon. Rather, he proposed, the only viable explanation was that the Book of Mormon had been dictated to Joseph Smith by a demon.

For about two weeks I simmered and pouted over that letter. In time I began to see things more clearly and realize that that may in fact be the only conclusion my friend can draw. Human explanations are too simplistic, by his own admission. And of course this all couldn't, simply couldn't, be of God. So there was only one option that made any sense—it was all of the devil. More recently, that same person said publicly: "I'm convinced (as are all who understand Scripture accurately) that Mormonism is a false religion, generated by Satan. It is a damnable heresy, and in the words of Paul, 'a different gospel,' under God's anathema."

As the apostle Paul taught, the things of God are known only by the power of the Spirit of God (see 1 Corinthians 2:11–14). The *truthfulness* of a religious matter is known by the quiet whisperings of the Spirit. But the *significance* of a religious matter—such as the Book of Mormon or temples or the nature of God—may often be discerned by the loud janglings of opposition that seem to flow naturally from those who are somehow offended by them. In other words, if I did not already know by the power of the Spirit that the Book of Mormon is indeed the word of God and Another Testament of Jesus Christ, I might suspect that it is holy writ by the intensity and even rabidity of those who attack it.

Nephi warned: "Wo be unto him that saith: We have received, and we need no more! And in fine, wo unto all those who tremble, and are angry because of the truth of God! For behold, he that is built upon the rock receiveth it with gladness" (2 Nephi 28:27–28). Do these verses—or any others I have quoted—bear the mark of the demonic? Do they produce behavior that is vile, sinful, immoral, or corrupt? If those who rail against the Book of Mormon would spend a fraction of their time and energy seeking to discover and fathom the *fruits* of the Book of Mormon as they do in conjuring up a new angle every month to explain the *roots* of it, they just might come to different conclusions. People must judge for themselves. As President Benson observed, "The Book of Mormon is not on trial—the people of the world, including the members of the Church, are on trial as to what they will do with this second witness for Christ."[19]

NEARER TO GOD

We are given little indication in the biblical record that the prophet-writers delivered and preserved their messages for any day other than their own. There is no doubt that Isaiah, Jeremiah, Ezekiel, Daniel, Malachi, Peter, Paul, John, and others spoke of the distant future; by the power of the Spirit, they saw and described the doings of peoples of another time and place. Their words were given to the people of their own time. Their words have found—and will yet find—application and fulfillment for other times. Yet we never see a particular prophet in the stick of Judah addressing himself directly to those who will one day read his pronouncements.

How very different is the Book of Mormon. It was prepared and preserved by men with seeric vision who wrote and spoke to us, who saw and knew our day and addressed themselves to specific issues that peoples in the last days would confront. The poignant words of Moroni assert to us the contemporary relevance of the Book of Mormon: "Behold, I speak unto you as if ye were present, and yet ye are not. But behold, Jesus Christ hath shown you unto me, and I know your doing" (Mormon 8:35). Later Moroni said: "Behold, I speak unto you as though I spake from the dead; for I know that ye shall have my words" (Mormon 9:30). In the words of President Ezra Taft Benson, the Book of Mormon "was written for our day. *The Nephites never had the book; neither did the Lamanites of ancient times.* It was meant for us. Mormon wrote near the end of the Nephite civilization. Under the inspiration of God, who sees all things from the beginning, he abridged centuries of records, choosing the stories, speeches, and events that would be most helpful to us. . . .

"If they saw our day, and chose those things which would be of greatest worth to us, is not that how we should study the Book of Mormon? We should constantly ask ourselves, 'Why did the Lord inspire Mormon (or Moroni or Alma) to include that in his record? What lesson can I learn from that to help me live in this day and age?'"[20]

Do I desire to know how to handle wayward children? How to deal justly yet mercifully with transgressors? How to bear pure testimony? How to teach and preach in such a manner that people cannot go away unaffected? How to detect the enemies of Christ and how to withstand those who seek to destroy my faith? How to discern and expose secret combinations that seek to destroy the works of the Lamb of God? How to deal properly with persecution and anti-Mormonism and how to establish Zion? Then I must search and study the Book of Mormon.

Do I desire to know more about how to avoid pride and the perils of the prosperity cycle? How to avoid priestcraft and acquire and embody charity, the pure love of Christ? How to have my sins remitted and how to know when they have been forgiven? How to retain a remission of sins from day to day? How to come unto Christ, receive his holy name, partake of his goodness and love, be sanctified by his Spirit, and eventually be sealed to him? How to prepare for the second coming of the Son of Man? Then I must search and study the Book of Mormon. This volume of holy writ is without equal. It is the most relevant and pertinent book available to humankind today.

The Book of Mormon is different from the other books of scripture that are also true and are also inspired. They too come from God. But the Book of Mormon has a spirit all its own. "Not all truths are of equal value," President Benson taught, "nor are all scriptures of the same worth." Moreover, "it is not just that the Book of Mormon teaches us truth, though it indeed does that. It is not just that the Book of Mormon bears testimony of Christ, though it indeed does that, too. But there is something more. There is a power in the book which will begin to flow into your lives the moment you begin a serious study of the book. You will find greater power to resist temptation. You will find the power to avoid deception. You will find the power to stay on the strait and narrow path. The scriptures are called 'the words of life' (D&C 84:85), and nowhere is that more true than it is of the Book of Mormon. When you begin to hunger and thirst after those words, you will find life in greater and greater abundance."[21]

The Book of Mormon is far more than a theological treatise, more than a collection of great doctrinal sermons. It is not just a book that helps us feel good; it is a heavenly document that has been given to help us *be* good. It is as if the Nephite prophet-leaders were beckoning and pleading to us from the dust: "We sought for the Lord. We found him. We applied the gospel of Jesus Christ and have partaken of its sweet fruits. We know the joy of our redemption and have felt to sing the song of redeeming love. And now, O reader, go thou and do likewise!"

The Book of Mormon is both an invitation to come unto Christ and a pattern for the accomplishment of that consummate privilege. That invitation is extended to all humankind, the rank and file as well as the prophets and apostles. The Book of Mormon does more than teach with plainness and persuasion the effects of the Fall and the absolute necessity for the Atonement; it cries out to us that unless we acknowledge our fallen state, put off the natural man, apply the atoning blood of Christ, and be born again, we can never be with or become like our Lord, worlds without end. Nor can we ever hope to establish Zion, a society of the pure in heart. Stated differently, the Book of Mormon is not just a book about religion; it *is* religion. Our challenge, therefore, is not just to read and study the Book of Mormon; we must live it and accept and apply its doctrines and philosophy.

A SERIOUS MATTER

Through the generations following the planting of the Lehite colony in America, leader after leader, prophets and kings, led this branch of Israel in truth and righteousness. Though they were inspired by a singular cause, their styles and their approaches to leadership no doubt varied. Yet one symbol and type remained constant: the military leaders among the Nephites wielded the sword of Laban in the defense of their people. That sword was a sign, an ensign, and an ever-present reminder that only through the Lord's divine assistance can individuals or nations be delivered from their enemies. It stood for something else as well—the price to be paid for scriptural, and thus spiritual, literacy. When the future Nephites needed the plates of brass to preserve their language and their religious integrity, a wicked man blocked the way. God thus commanded that this man's blood be shed so that the sacred record could be obtained by Nephi. The scriptures are always bought with a price (see 1 Nephi 3).

And so it is in regard to the Book of Mormon itself. Too much effort has been expended over too many centuries, too much blood has been shed, too many tears have watered too many pillows, too many prayers have ascended to the ears of the Lord of Sabaoth, too great a price has been paid for the Book of Mormon record to be destroyed. Or discarded. Or ignored. No, it must not be ignored, either by the Latter-day Saints (the present custodians of the stick of Joseph) or by a world that desperately needs its message and transforming power.

No less a being than God himself has borne witness of the Book of Mormon. To Oliver Cowdery, who was raised up to serve as scribe in the translation, the Lord affirmed: "I tell thee, that thou mayest know that there is none else save God that knowest thy thoughts and intents of thy heart. I tell thee these things as a witness unto thee—that *the words or the work which thou hast been writing are true*" (D&C 6:16–17; italics added; compare 18:2). The Almighty set his own seal of truthfulness upon the Nephite record by an oath when he said: "And he [Joseph Smith] has translated the book, even that part which I have commanded him, and *as your Lord and your God liveth it is true*" (D&C 17:6; italics added). In the words of a modern apostle: "This is God's testimony of the Book of Mormon. In it Deity himself has laid his godhood on the line. Either the book is true or God ceases to be God. There neither is nor can be any more formal or powerful language known to men or gods."[22]

For those outside the faith, the Book of Mormon presses for a decision. One cannot simply dismiss it with a wave of the hand and a turn of the head. It must be explained. Thus Elder Bruce R. McConkie declared: "The time is long past for quibbling about words and for hurling unsavory epithets against the Latter-day Saints. These are deep and solemn and ponderous matters. We need not think we can trifle with sacred things and escape the wrath of a just God.

"Either the Book of Mormon is true, or it is false; either it came from God, or it was spawned in the infernal realms. . . . It is not and cannot be simply another treatise on religion; it either came from heaven or from hell. And it is time for all those who seek salvation to find out for themselves whether it is of the Lord or of Lucifer."[23]

As for members of the Church, President Ezra Taft Benson declared boldly: "Every Latter-day Saint should make the study of this book a lifetime pursuit. Otherwise he is placing his soul in jeopardy and neglecting that which could give spiritual and intellectual unity to his whole life."[24]

CONCLUSION

In compliance with prophetic mandate, millions of Latter-day Saints across the world have begun to search and pray over and teach from the Book of Mormon. Because of their study of the Book of Mormon, many Saints are already finding answers to their problems; many Saints have come alive to the scriptures and have begun to understand the more mysterious passages in the Bible. Many have begun to feel that subtle but certain transforming influence that flows from the Book of Mormon—they have begun to sense its sanctifying power. Theirs is a greater yearning for righteousness and the things of the Spirit, a heightened sensitivity to people and feelings, and a corresponding abhorrence for the sins of the world. Many have come to the point where they honestly and truly desire to surrender to the Lord and his ways, to know and abide by his will, and to keep an eye single to his glory. For such devotees of the Book of Mormon, surely the condemnation spoken of in Doctrine and Covenants 84 is no more.

I believe this pattern will continue and this movement will grow. President Benson said: "I have a vision of homes alerted, of classes alive, and of pulpits aflame with the spirit of Book of Mormon messages.

"I have a vision of home teachers and visiting teachers, ward and branch officers, and stake and mission leaders counseling our people out of the most correct of any book on earth—the Book of Mormon.

"I have a vision of artists putting into film, drama, literature, music, and paintings great themes and great characters from the Book of Mormon.

"I have a vision of thousands of missionaries going into the mission field with hundreds of passages memorized from the Book of Mormon so that they might feed the needs of a spiritually famished world.

"I have a vision of the whole Church getting nearer to God by abiding by the precepts of the Book of Mormon.

"Indeed, I have a vision of flooding the earth with the Book of Mormon."[25]

The day is within reach when the Lord's words—as found in the Book of Mormon—shall hiss forth unto the ends of the earth for a standard unto the Lord's people, the house of Israel (2 Nephi 29:2). The covenant people of the Lord who are scattered among the nations will respond to that voice from the dust that speaks with a familiar spirit. Multitudes of our Father's children will gather to Christ and thereafter to the lands of their inheritance through the Book of Mormon. All nations will, as the ancients foresaw, gather to the mountain of the Lord's house—to the stakes of Zion and to the covenants and ordinances of the holy temple— in preparation for the establishment of the New Jerusalem. The Book of Mormon will play an integral role in that process. The Prophet Joseph Smith's inspired translation of the Bible tells of the role the Book of Mormon will play in the final winding-up scenes:

"And the Lord said unto Enoch: As I live, even so will I come in the last days, in the days of wickedness and vengeance, to fulfil the oath which I have made unto you concerning the children of Noah;

"And the day shall come that the earth shall rest, but before that day the heavens shall be darkened, and a veil of darkness shall cover the earth; and the heavens shall shake, and also the earth; and great tribulations shall be among the children of men, but my people will I preserve;

"And righteousness will I send down out of heaven; and *truth will I send forth out of the earth, to bear testimony of mine Only*

Begotten; his resurrection from the dead; yea, and also the resurrection of all men; and righteousness and truth will I cause to sweep the earth as with a flood, to gather out mine elect from the four quarters of the earth, unto a place which I shall prepare, an Holy City, that my people may gird up their loins, and be looking forth for the time of my coming; for there shall be my tabernacle, and it shall be called Zion, a New Jerusalem" (Moses 7:60–62; emphasis added).

But such a scene will not come to pass without opposition. Ignorance and prejudice now abound among many, just as love and light and pure religion will abound among those who accept and build their lives upon the rock of revealed religion. Antipathy to Joseph Smith, to the Book of Mormon, and to the Latter-day Saints will increase. But amid it all, the work of the Lord, with the Book of Mormon held high as an ensign to the nations, will go forward. Moroni explained to Joseph Smith: "Those who are not built upon the Rock will seek to overthrow this church; but it will increase the more [it is] opposed."[26]

We are not far removed from a deeply significant era in this final dispensation, a time seen in vision by Nephi: "And it came to pass that I beheld that the great mother of abominations did gather together multitudes upon the face of all the earth, among all the nations of the Gentiles, to fight against the Lamb of God. And it came to pass that I, Nephi, beheld the power of the Lamb of God, that it descended upon the saints of the church of the Lamb, and upon the covenant people of the Lord, who were scattered upon all the face of the earth; and they were armed with righteousness and with the power of God in great glory" (1 Nephi 14:13–14).

I know that the Book of Mormon is the word of God. I know that the Lord God is its author. It speaks peace and joy to my soul. It is a quiet, steadying influence in my life. Many of our longings for another time and place, those vague but powerful feelings that we have "wandered from a more exalted sphere," are satisfied and soothed when we read the Book of Mormon (*Hymns,* no. 292). Reading it is like coming home. It is a gift of God that we are expected to receive, understand, and experience. I feel a deep sense of kinship with its writers, particularly Mormon and Moroni. I know they are as concerned now, if not more, with what is done with their book than they were when they etched their messages onto the golden plates some sixteen centuries ago. I know that the Almighty expects us to read and teach from the Book of Mormon and to devote significant time to the consideration and application of the doctrines and principles it contains.

President Gordon B. Hinckley declared: "Its appeal is as timeless as truth, as universal as mankind. It is the only book that contains within its covers a promise that by divine power the reader may know with certainty of its truth.

"Its origin is miraculous; when the story of that origin is first told to one unfamiliar with it, it is almost unbelievable. But the book is here to be felt and handled and read. No one can dispute its presence. All efforts to account for its origin, other than the account given by Joseph Smith, have been shown to lack substance. It is a record of ancient America. It is a scripture of the New World, as certainly as the Bible is the scripture of the Old. Each speaks of the other. Each carries with it the spirit of inspiration, the power to convince and convert. Together they become two witnesses, hand in hand, that Jesus is the Christ, the resurrected and living Son of the living God."[27]

God grant that we might be wise in the day of our probation. God grant us strength in our sacred care and keeping of the timely and timeless Book of Mormon. Then, having done all in this regard, we will rest our souls everlastingly with those who paid such a dear price to write and preserve and bring it forth.

CHAPTER THREE

LIVING DOCTRINE

The central, saving doctrine of our faith is that Jesus is the Christ, the Son of God, the Savior and Redeemer of humankind; that he lived, taught, healed, suffered and died for our sins; and that he rose from the dead the third day with a glorious, immortal, resurrected body (1 Corinthians 15:1–3; D&C 76:40–42). The Prophet Joseph Smith spoke of these central truths as the "fundamental principles" of our religion to which all other doctrines are but appendages.[1] Elder Boyd K. Packer taught: "Truth, glorious truth, proclaims there is . . . a Mediator. . . .

"Through Him mercy can be fully extended to each of us without offending the eternal law of justice.

"*This truth is the very root of Christian doctrine.* You may know much about the gospel as it branches out from there, but *if you only know the branches and those branches do not touch that root,* if they have been cut free from that truth, *there will be no life nor substance nor redemption in them.*"[2]

There is power in doctrine, power in the word (Alma 31:5), power to heal the wounded soul (Jacob 2:8), power to transform human behavior. We are under obligation to learn the doctrines, teach them properly, and bind ourselves to speak and act in harmony with them. Only in this way can we perpetuate truth in a world filled with error, avoid deception, focus on what matters most, and find joy and happiness in the process. "I have spoken before about the importance of keeping the doctrine of the Church pure, and seeing that it is taught in all of our meetings," President Gordon B. Hinckley stated. "I worry about this. Small aberrations in doctrinal teaching can lead to large and evil falsehoods."[3]

How do we "keep the doctrine pure"? What might we do?

1. We can teach directly from the scriptures, the standard works. The scriptures contain the mind and will and voice and word of the Lord (D&C 68:3–4) to men and women in earlier days and thus doctrine and applications that are both timely and time-less. "All Scripture given by inspiration of God, is profitable for doctrine, for reproof, for correction, for instruction in righteousness; that the man [or woman] of God may be perfect, thoroughly furnished unto all good works" (JST 2 Timothy 3:16–17).

2. We can present the doctrine in the same way the prophets in our own day present it (D&C 52:9, 36), in both content and emphasis. Mormon wrote: "And it came to pass that Alma, having authority from God, organized priests; . . . and he commanded them that *they should teach nothing save it were the things which he had taught*" (Mosiah 18:18–19; emphasis added). "Therefore they did assemble themselves together in different bodies, being called churches; every church having their priests and their teachers, and *every priest teaching the word according as it was delivered to him by the mouth of Alma*. And thus, notwithstanding there being many churches they were all one church, yea, even the church of God" (Mosiah 25:21–22; emphasis added).

3. We can pay special attention to the scriptural commentary offered by living apostles and prophets in general conference

addresses, cross-reference it into our scriptures, and teach this commentary in conjunction with the scripture.

4. We can teach the gospel with plainness and simplicity, focus on fundamentals, and emphasize what matters most. We do not tell all we know, nor do we teach on the edge of our knowledge. The Prophet Joseph Smith explained that "it is not always wise to relate all the truth. Even Jesus, the Son of God, had to refrain from doing so, and had to restrain His feelings many times for the safety of Himself and His followers, and had to conceal the righteous purposes of His heart in relation to many things pertaining to His Father's kingdom."[4]

5. We can acknowledge that there are some things we simply do not know. President Joseph F. Smith declared: "It is no discredit to our intelligence or to our integrity to say frankly in the face of a hundred speculative questions, 'I do not know.'

"One thing is certain, and that is, God has revealed enough to our understanding for our exaltation and for our happiness. Let the Saints, then, utilize what they already have; be simple and unaffected in their religion, both in thought and word, and they will not easily lose their bearings and be subjected to the vain philosophies of man."[5]

DISCERNING TRUE DOCTRINE

A Baptist minister visited me at my office one day. As we chatted about a number of things, including doctrine, he said, "Bob, you people believe in such strange things!"

"Like what?" I asked.

"Oh, for example," he said, "you believe in blood atonement. And that affects Utah's insistence on retaining capital punishment by a firing squad."

I responded, "No, we don't."

"Yes, you do," he came right back. "I know of several statements by Brigham Young, Heber C. Kimball, and Jedediah Grant that teach such things."

"I'm aware of those statements," I said. I then found myself saying something that I had never voiced before: "Yes, those statements were made, but *they do not represent the doctrine of our Church.* We believe in the blood atonement of Jesus Christ and that alone."

My friend didn't miss a beat: "What do you mean they don't represent the doctrine of your Church? They were spoken by major Church leaders."

I explained that such statements were made, for the most part, during the time of the Mormon Reformation, and they are examples of a kind of "revival rhetoric" through which the leaders of the Church were striving to "raise the bar" of the Saints' obedience and faithfulness. I assured him that the Church, by its own canonical standards, does not have the right or the authority to take a person's life because of disobedience or even apostasy (D&C 134:10). I read to him a passage from the Book of Mormon in which the Nephite prophets had resorted to "exceeding harshness, . . . continually reminding [the people] of death, and the duration of eternity, and the judgments and the power of God, . . . and exceedingly great plainness of speech" in order to "keep them from going down speedily to destruction" (Enos 1:23).

He seemed satisfied to some extent, but then he said, "Bob, many of my fellow Christians have noted that it is hard to figure out what Mormons believe. They say it's like trying to nail green Jell-O to the wall! What *do* you people believe? How *do* you decide what is your doctrine and what is not?"

I suggested that he consider the following three ideas:

1. The teachings of the Church today have a rather narrow focus, range, and direction; central and saving doctrine is what we

are called upon to teach and emphasize, not tangential and peripheral matters.

2. Very often what is drawn from Church leaders of the past is,
like the matter of blood atonement, misquoted, misrepresented, or
taken out of context. Further, not everything that was ever spoken
or written by a Church leader in the past is a part of what we teach
today. Ours is a living constitution, a living tree of life, a dynamic
Church (D&C 1:30). We are commanded to pay heed to the words
of living oracles (D&C 90:3–5).

3. In determining whether something is a part of the doctrine
of the Church, we might ask: Is it found within the four standard
works? Within official declarations or proclamations? Is it taught
or discussed in general conference or other official gatherings by
general Church leaders today? Is it found in the general handbooks
or approved curriculum of the Church today?[6] If it meets at least
one of these criteria, we can feel secure and appropriate about
teaching it. We might also add that included within the category of
"all that God does reveal" would be certain matters that fall under
the injunction to maintain "sacred silence." For example, the content of the temple endowment today would certainly be considered
a part of the doctrine of the Church.

A significant proportion of anti-Mormonism focuses on statements by Church leaders of the past that deal with peripheral
issues. No one criticizes us for a belief in God; in the divinity of
Jesus Christ or his atoning work; in the literal, bodily resurrection
of the Savior and the eventual resurrection of humankind; in baptism by immersion; in the gift of the Holy Ghost; the sacrament of
the Lord's Supper, etc. In that spirit, we must never allow a person
not of our faith to teach us—to insist upon—what *we* believe. If as
an active, practicing member of The Church of Jesus Christ of
Latter-day Saints, I do not have the right to introduce or declare

doctrine, why should someone from outside my faith be allowed to do so?

We love the scriptures and thank God for them, and yet we believe that one can have sufficient confidence in and even reverence for holy writ without believing that every word between Genesis 1:1 and Revelation 22:21 is the word-for-word dictation of the Almighty or that the Bible now reads as it has always read. Indeed, our scriptures attest that plain and precious truths and many covenants of the Lord were taken away or kept back from the Bible before it was compiled (1 Nephi 13:20–29; Moses 1:40–41; Articles of Faith 1:8).[7] But we still cherish the sacred volume, recognize and teach the doctrines of salvation within it, and seek to pattern our lives according to its timeless teachings.

In like manner, we can sustain with all our hearts the prophets and apostles without believing that they are perfect or that everything they say or do is exactly what God wants said or done. In short, we do not believe in apostolic or prophetic infallibility. Moses made mistakes, but we love him and accept his prophetic writings nonetheless. Peter made mistakes, but we honor him and study his words. Paul made mistakes, but we admire his boldness and dedication and treasure his epistles. James pointed out that Elijah "was a man subject to like passions as we are" (James 5:17), and the Prophet Joseph Smith taught that "a prophet [is] a prophet only when he [is] acting as such."[8]

On another occasion the Prophet declared: "I told them I was but a man, and they must not expect me to be perfect; if they expected perfection from me, I should expect it from them; but if they would bear with my infirmities and the infirmities of the brethren, I would likewise bear with their infirmities."[9]

"I can fellowship the President of the Church," said Lorenzo Snow, "if he does not know everything I know. . . . I saw the . . . imperfections in [Joseph Smith]. . . . I thanked God that He would put upon a man who had those imperfections the power and authority He placed upon him . . . for I knew that I myself had weakness, and I thought there was a chance for me."[10]

Individual members of the Church, including those called to guide its destiny, have the right to be wrong at one time or another—to say something that simply isn't true. They also have the right to improve their views, to change their minds and correct mistakes as new light and new truth become available.

As we have been reminded again and again, whom God calls, God qualifies. God calls his prophets. He empowers and strengthens the individual, provides an eternal perspective, loosens his tongue and enables him to make known divine truth. But being called as an apostle or even as president of the Church does not remove the man's mortality or make him perfect. President David O. McKay explained that "when God makes the prophet He does not unmake the man."[11]

"I was this morning introduced to a man from the east," Joseph Smith stated. "After hearing my name, he remarked that I was nothing but a man, indicating by this expression, that he had supposed that a person to whom the Lord would see fit to reveal His will, must be something more than a man. He seemed to have forgotten the saying that fell from the lips of St. James, that [Elijah] was a man subject to like passions as we are, yet he had such power with God, that He, in answer to his prayers, shut the heavens that they gave no rain for the space of three years and six months."[12]

President Gordon B. Hinckley stated: "I have worked with seven Presidents of this Church. I have recognized that all have been human. But I have never been concerned over this. They may have had some weaknesses. But this has never troubled me. I know that the God of heaven has used mortal men throughout history to accomplish His divine purposes."[13] On another occasion President Hinckley pleaded with the Saints that "as we continue our search for truth . . . we look for strength and goodness rather than weakness and foibles in those who did so great a work in their time.

"We recognize that our forebears were human. They doubtless made mistakes. . . .

"There was only one perfect man who ever walked the earth. The Lord has used imperfect people in the process of building his perfect society. If some of them occasionally stumbled, or if their characters may have been slightly flawed in one way or another, the wonder is the greater that they accomplished so much."[14]

TOUGH ISSUES

Some time ago a colleague and I spoke in southern California to a group of about five hundred Latter-day Saints and Protestants. During the question-and-answer phase of the program, someone asked me the inevitable question: "Are you really Christian? Do you, as many claim, worship a different Jesus?"

I answered that we worship the Christ of the New Testament, that we believe wholeheartedly in his virgin birth, his divine Sonship, his miracles, his transforming teachings, his atoning sacrifice, and his bodily resurrection from the dead. I added that we also believe in the teachings of and about Christ found in the Book of Mormon and modern revelation.

After the meeting an LDS woman came up to me and said, "You didn't tell the truth about what we believe!"

Startled, I asked, "What do you mean?"

She responded, "You said we believe in the virgin birth of Christ, and you know very well that we don't believe that."

"Yes, we do," I retorted.

She then said with a great deal of emotion, "I want to believe you, but people have told me for years that we believe that God the Father had sexual relations with Mary and thereby Jesus was conceived." I looked her in the eyes and said, "I'm aware of that teaching, but that is not the doctrine of the Church; that is not what we teach in the Church today. Have you ever heard the Brethren teach it in conference? Is it in the standard works, the curricular materials, or the handbooks of the Church? Is it a part of an official declaration or proclamation?" I watched as an enormous weight seemed to come off her shoulders. Tears came into her eyes, and she simply said, "Thank you, Brother Millet."

Once Pastor Greg Johnson and I met with the members of an Evangelical Christian church just outside Salt Lake City. The minister asked us to come and make a presentation ("An Evangelical and a Latter-day Saint in Dialogue") that Greg and I have made scores of times in various parts of the country. The whole purpose of our presentation is to model the kind of relationships people with differing religious views can have. This kind of presentation has proven to be one of the most effective bridge-building exercises in which I have been involved.

On that particular night, the first question asked by someone in the audience was on DNA and the Book of Mormon. I commented briefly, indicating that a more detailed (and informed) response would be forthcoming soon in a journal article by a BYU biologist.

Many, many hands were in the air. I called on a woman close to the front. She asked, "How do you deal with the Adam-God doctrine?"

I responded, "Thank you for that question. It gives me an opportunity to explain a principle mentioned early in our exchange that lays the foundation for other things to be said." I took a few moments to address the questions, "What is our doctrine? What do we teach today?" I indicated that if some teaching or idea was not in the standard works, not among official declarations or proclamations, was not taught currently by living apostles or prophets in general conference or other official gatherings, or was not in the general handbooks or official curriculum of the Church, it is probably *not* a part of the doctrine or teachings of the Church.

I was surprised when my pastor friend said to the group: "Are you listening? Do you hear what Bob is saying? This is important! It's time for us to stop criticizing Latter-day Saints on matters they don't even teach today."

Two things happened immediately. First, the hands of many questioners went down, and second, the tone of the meeting changed dramatically. The questions became not baiting or challenging but rather efforts to clarify. The last question was asked by a middle-aged man. He stood up and said: "I for one would like to thank you, from the bottom of my heart, for what you have done here tonight. This thrills my soul. I think this is what Jesus would do. I have lived in Utah for many years, and I have many LDS friends. We get along okay; we don't fight and quarrel over religious matters. But we really don't talk with one another about things that matter most to us, that is, our faith. I don't plan to become a Latter-day Saint, and I'm certain my Mormon friends don't plan to become Evangelical, but I would like to find more effective ways to talk heart to heart. Could you two make a few suggestions on how we can deepen and sweeten our relationships with our LDS neighbors?"

These experiences highlight for me the challenge we face. I have no hesitation telling an individual or a group "I don't know" when I am asked why men are ordained to the priesthood and women are not, why blacks were denied the blessings of the priesthood for almost a century and a half, and several other matters that have neither been revealed nor clarified by those holding the proper keys. The difficulty comes when someone in the past *has* spoken on these matters, *has* put forward ideas that are out of harmony with what we know and teach today, and when those teachings are still available, either in print or among the everyday conversations of the members, and have never been corrected or clarified. The questions underlying all of this are simply "What is our doctrine? What are the teachings of the Church today?" If the Saints (and the larger religious world) could understand the answers to those questions, our missionary effort, our convert retention, our activation, and the image and overall strength of the Church would be enhanced. If presented properly, the answers need not weaken faith or create doubts. It could do much to focus the Saints more on the central, saving verities of the gospel.

Some who are told that not everything stated by a latter-day prophet or apostle is a part of the doctrine of the Church and of what we teach today may ask, "Well then, what *else* did this Church leader teach that is not considered doctrine today? How can we confidently accept anything else he taught? What other directions taken or procedures pursued by the Church in an earlier time do we not follow in our day?"

The answer is to refrain from taking such an approach. To take such a position is like throwing out the baby with the bath water. We must never allow ourselves to overgeneralize and thus over-react. Nor must we be guilty of discounting all that is good and uplifting and divinely given because of an aberration. After all, because a prophet once expressed an opinion or perhaps even put forward a view that needed further clarification or even correction, does not invalidate all else that he did or said. I would certainly hate to be judged that way and have no desire to be guilty of doing the same to the Lord's anointed. God calls his prophets, and God corrects them. He knows their strengths, and he knows their weaknesses.

Those of other faiths who leap to criticize the Church and question its truthfulness because of past teachings from Church leaders that are not accepted as doctrine today would do well to ask themselves if they are prepared to apply the same standards of judgment to their own tradition, their own prominent speakers, or their own past. This is like asking, "Would you like to better understand Roman Catholicism today? Then study carefully the atrocities of the Crusades or the horrors of the Inquisition." Or, "Would you like a deeper glimpse into the hearts of Lutherans today? Then make it your business to study the anti-Semitic writings of Martin Luther." Or, "Would you care to better understand Southern Baptists? Then simply read the many sermons during the Civil War of Baptist preachers who used biblical passages to justify the practice of slavery."

True doctrine has what might be called "sticking power"—it is taught and discussed and perpetuated over time, and with the passing of years seems to take on greater significance. Time, experience, careful and pondering thought, and subsequent revelation through prophets—these all either reinforce and support or bring into question and eventually discount a particular idea. To the Latter-day Saints the Lord Jesus declared: "And I give unto you a commandment, that ye shall forsake all evil and cleave unto all good, that ye shall live by every word which proceedeth forth out of the mouth of God. For he will give unto the faithful line upon line, precept upon precept; and I will try you and prove you herewith" (D&C 98:11–12; compare Isaiah 28:9–10; 2 Nephi 28:30).

One way to keep our doctrine pure is to present the gospel message the way the prophets and apostles today present it. Similarly, our explanations of certain "hard" doctrines or deeper doctrines should not go beyond what the prophets believe and teach today. Let's consider two illustrations.

The first is an extremely sensitive matter, one that continues to affect convert baptisms in the Church. I speak of the matter of blacks and the priesthood. I was raised in the Church and was well aware of the priesthood restriction. For as long as I can remember, the explanation for why our black brethren and sisters were denied the full blessings of the priesthood (including those of the temple) was some variation of the theme that they had been less valiant in the premortal life and thus had come to earth under a curse, an explanation that was perpetuated as doctrine for most of our Church's history. I had memorized the Article of Faith that states that we will be punished for our own sins and not for Adam's transgression and later read that "the sins of the parents cannot be answered upon the heads of the children" (Moses 6:54), but I had assumed that these principles somehow did not apply to the blacks.

In June 1978 everything changed—not just the matter of who could be ordained to the priesthood but also the explanation for why the restriction had been in place from the beginning. Elder Dallin H. Oaks was asked in a 1988 interview: "As much as any doctrine the Church has espoused, or controversy the Church has been embroiled in, this one [the priesthood restriction] seems to stand out. Church members seemed to have less to go on to get a grasp of the issue. Can you address why this was the case, and what can be learned from it?"

Elder Oaks responded: "If you read the scriptures with this question in mind, 'Why did the Lord command this or why did he command that,' you find that in less than one in a hundred commands was any reason given. It's not the pattern of the Lord to give reasons. We can put reason to revelation. We can put reasons to commandments. When we do we're on our own. Some people put reasons to the one we're talking about here, and they turned out to be spectacularly wrong. There is a lesson in that. The lesson I've drawn from that [is that] I decided a long time ago that I had faith in the command and I had no faith in the reasons that had been suggested for it."

Then came the follow-up question: "Are you referring to reasons given even by general authorities?"

Elder Oaks answered: "Sure. I'm referring to reasons given by general authorities and reasons elaborated upon that reason by others. The whole set of reasons seemed to me to be unnecessary risk-taking. . . . Let's don't make the mistake that's been made in the past, here and in other areas, trying to put reasons to revelation. The reasons turn out to be man-made to a great extent. The revelations are what we sustain as the will of the Lord and that's where safety lies."[15]

In other words, we do not know why the restriction on the priesthood existed. "I don't know" is the correct answer when we are asked why that restriction existed. It was restricted "for reasons which we believe are known to God, but which he has not made fully known to man."[16] That is what Elder Bruce R. McConkie meant in his August 1978 address to the Church Educational System when he counseled us to "forget everything that I have said, or what President Brigham Young or President George Q. Cannon or whosoever has said in days past that is contrary to the present revelation. We spoke with a limited understanding and without the light and knowledge that now has come into the world.

"We get our truth and our light line upon line and precept upon precept. We have now had added a new flood of intelligence and light on this particular subject, and it erases all the darkness and all the views and all the thoughts of the past. They don't matter any more. . . .

"It is a new day and a new arrangement, and the Lord has now given the revelation that sheds light out into the world on this subject. As to any slivers of light or any particles of darkness of the past, we forget about them."[17]

Now for the second illustration. I think I have never responded to questions from a group of persons not of our faith that I have not been asked about our doctrine of God and the Godhead, particularly the teachings of Joseph Smith and Lorenzo Snow. I generally do not have much difficulty explaining our view of how through the Atonement mankind can eventually become more and more Christlike, more like God. For that matter, Orthodox Christianity, a huge segment of the Christian world, still holds to a view of theosis, or human deification. The Bible itself teaches that men and women may become "partakers of the divine nature" (2 Peter 1:4), "joint-heirs with Christ" (Romans 8:17), gain "the mind of Christ" (1 Corinthians 2:16), and become perfect, even as our Father in Heaven is perfect (Matthew 5:48). The apostle John declared, "Beloved, now are we the sons [children] of God, and it doth not yet appear what we shall be: but we know that, when he shall appear, we shall be like him; for we shall see him as he is" (1 John 3:2). This doctrine is taught powerfully in modern revelation (D&C 76:58; 132:19–20).

The tougher issue for many Christians to deal with is the accompanying doctrine set forth in the King Follett Sermon[18] and the Lorenzo Snow couplet[19]—namely, that God was once a man. Latter-day scriptures state unequivocally that God is a man, a Man of Holiness (Moses 6:57) who possesses a body of flesh and bones (D&C 130:22). These concepts are clearly a part of the doctrinal restoration. We teach that man is not of a lower order or of a different species than God. That makes many of our Christian friends extremely uncomfortable, for it appears to them that we are lowering God in the scheme of things and thus attempting to bridge the Creator-creature chasm.

We can say in response to their concern that we know what we know as a result of modern revelation and that from our perspective, the distance between God and man is still immeasurable. Our Father in Heaven is indeed omnipotent, omniscient, and, by the power of his Holy Spirit, omnipresent. He is a glorified, exalted, resurrected being, "the only supreme governor and independent being in whom all fulness and perfection dwell; . . . in him every good gift and every good principle dwell; . . . he is the Father of lights; in him the principle of faith dwells independently, and he is the object in whom the faith of all other rational and accountable beings center for life and salvation."[20] Modern revelation attests that the Almighty sits enthroned "with glory, honor, power, majesty, might, dominion, truth, justice, judgment, mercy, and an infinity of fulness" (D&C 109:77).

And what do we know beyond the truth that God is an exalted Man? What do we know of his mortal existence? What do we know of the time before he became God? Nothing. We do not know more than was stated by the Prophet Joseph Smith, and that is precious little. Insights concerning God's life before Godhood are not found in the standard works, in official declarations or proclamations, in current handbooks or curricular materials, nor are doctrinal expositions on the subject delivered in general conference today. This topic is not what we would call a central and saving doctrine, one that must be believed (or understood) in order to hold a temple recommend or be in good standing in the Church.

This second illustration highlights an important point: *Doctrine* means "teaching." If the general authorities do not teach something today, it is not part of our doctrine today. This does not, however, mean that a particular teaching is untrue. A teaching may be true and yet not a part of what is taught and emphasized in the Church today. Whether it is true or not may be irrelevant, if indeed the Brethren do not teach it today or it is not taught directly in the standard works or found in our correlated curriculum. For example, consider the question, Was Jesus married? The scriptures do not provide an answer. "We do not know anything about Jesus Christ being married," President Charles W. Penrose stated. "The Church has no authoritative declaration on the subject."[21] So whether he was or was not married is not part of the doctrine of the Church. In such cases it would be well to apply the following lesson from President Harold B. Lee: "With respect to doctrines and meanings of scriptures, let me give you a safe counsel. It is usually not well to use a single passage of scripture [or a single sermon] in proof of a point of doctrine unless it is confirmed by modern revelation or by the Book of Mormon. . . . To single out a passage of scripture to prove a point, unless it is [so] confirmed . . . is always a hazardous thing."[22]

CONCLUSION

The Lord stated to Joseph Smith in Nauvoo: "I deign to reveal unto my church things which have been kept hid from before the foundation of the world, things that pertain to the dispensation of the fulness of times" (D&C 124:41; compare 121:26; 128:18). I tell my students frequently that it is as important for us to know *what we do not know* as it is for us to know what we know. Far too many things are taught or discussed or even argued that fit into the realm of the unrevealed and thus the unresolved. Such matters, particularly if they do not fall within the range of revealed truth we teach today, do not edify or inspire. Often, very often, they lead to confusion and sow discord.

This does not in any way mean that we should not seek to study and grow and expand in our gospel understanding. Peter explained that there needs to be a reason for the hope within us (1 Peter 3:15). Our knowledge should be as settling to the mind as it is soothing to the heart. Elder Neal A. Maxwell taught that some "Church members know just enough about the doctrines to converse superficially on them, but their scant knowledge about the deep doctrines is inadequate for deep discipleship. (See 1 Corinthians 2:10.) Thus uninformed about the deep doctrines, they make no deep change in their lives."[23] President Hugh B. Brown once observed: "I am impressed with the testimony of a man who can stand and say he knows the gospel is true. What I would like to ask is 'But, sir, do you know the gospel?' . . . Mere testimony can be gained with but perfunctory knowledge of the Church and its teachings. . . . But to retain a testimony, to be of service in building the Lord's kingdom, requires a serious study of the gospel and knowing what it is."[24] Again, the issue is one of focus, one of emphasis—where we choose to spend our time when we teach the gospel to Latter-day Saints and to individuals of other faiths.

There is a valid reason why it may seem difficult to "tie down" Latter-day Saint doctrine, one that derives from the very nature of the Restoration. The truth that God continues to speak through his anointed servants; that he, through those servants, continues to reveal, elucidate, and clarify what has already been given; and that our canon of scripture is open, flexible, and expanding—all of this militates against what many in the Christian world would call a systematic theology.

Elder Maxwell explained, "Deeds *do* matter as well as doctrines, but the doctrines can move us to do the deeds, and the Spirit can help us to understand the doctrines as well as prompt us to do the deeds."[25] He also noted that "when weary legs falter and detours and roadside allurements entice, the fundamental doctrines will summon from deep within us fresh determination. Extraordinary truths can move us to extraordinary accomplishments!"[26] The teaching and application of sound doctrine are great safeguards to us in these last days, shields against the fiery darts of the adversary. Understanding true doctrine and being true to that doctrine can keep us from ignorance, from error, and from sin. It is the declaration of sound and solid doctrine, the doctrine found in scripture and taught by living oracles that builds faith and strengthens testimony and commitment to the Lord and his kingdom.

CHAPTER FOUR

CHRIST'S ETERNAL GOSPEL

The scriptures of the Restoration and latter-day prophets affirm that God our Father has a plan for his children, a program established to maximize our growth and ensure our happiness. And yet that truth alone—that there is some divine plan to life—is not as obvious from the Bible as it is from latter-day scripture. Knowing what we know from modern revelation, we are able to recognize divine design, but seldom can we turn to a specific Old or New Testament passage that speaks with clarity of a plan. How very different is the Book of Mormon! The Nephite prophets speak with grateful hearts for the merciful plan of the great Creator (2 Nephi 9:6), the plan of our God (2 Nephi 9:13), the great plan of mercy (Alma 42:15, 31), the plan of redemption (Jacob 6:8; Alma 12:25–26, 30, 32; 17:16; 18:39; 22:13–14; 29:2; 34:31; 39:18; 42:11, 13), the eternal plan of deliverance (2 Nephi 11:5), the plan of salvation (Jarom 1:2; Alma 24:14; 42:5), and the great plan of happiness (Alma 42:8, 16). We know that the plan of salvation is "always and everlastingly the same; that obedience to the same laws always brings the same reward; that the gospel laws have not changed . . . ; and that always and everlastingly all things pertaining to salvation center in Christ."[1]

AN ETERNAL ATONEMENT

Jesus is truly the "Lamb slain from the foundation of the world" (Revelation 13:8; Moses 7:47). That is, the atoning sacrifice is not just timely (for all who need its cleansing powers) but *timeless.* Though the act of atonement would not take place until Jesus suffered in Gethsemane and on Golgotha in the meridian of time, earth's earliest inhabitants were taught to call upon God in the name of his Beloved Son for deliverance (Moses 5:5–8). Again, this central truth is not to be had in traditional Christendom. Indeed, one fascinating attack on the Book of Mormon is that it is too Christ-centered! That is, critics contend, the Book of Mormon has too much of Christ within it, long before there was a Christ.

We know that God has revealed himself, his plan, and the Mediator of his sacred covenant to his children from the beginning. The voice of the Father came to Adam: "If thou wilt turn unto me, and hearken unto my voice, and believe, and repent of all thy transgressions, and be baptized, even in water, in the name of mine Only Begotten Son . . . , which is Jesus Christ, the only name which shall be given under heaven, whereby salvation shall come unto the children of men, ye shall receive the gift of the Holy Ghost" (Moses 6:52). Further, Adam was commanded to teach his children that all men and women, because of the effects of the Fall, "must be born again into the kingdom of heaven, of water, and of the Spirit, and be cleansed by blood, even the blood of mine Only Begotten; that ye might be sanctified from all sin, and enjoy the words of eternal life in this world, and eternal life in the world to come, even immortal glory" (Moses 6:59).

The Prophet Joseph Smith observed that "we cannot believe that the ancients in all ages were so ignorant of the system of heaven as many suppose, since all that were ever saved, were saved through the power of this great plan of redemption, as much before the coming of Christ as since; if not, God has had different plans in operation (if we may so express it), to bring men back to dwell with Himself; and this we cannot believe, since there has been no change in the constitution of man since he fell."[2] And so it is that we learn through the scriptures of the Restoration that, in addition to Adam, such prophetic personalities from the Bible as Enoch (Moses 7), Noah (Moses 8), Abraham (JST Genesis 15:9–12), and Moses (Moses 1) received revelation concerning the particulars of the Father's plan, and they knew and taught of the coming redemption in Jesus Christ. Truly, as the apostle Peter proclaimed, "To [Christ] give all the prophets witness" (Acts 10:43).

It was no different in the western hemisphere. With Lehi and his family came the fulness of the gospel, including the holy priesthood, the knowledge of salvation, and the intercessory role of Jesus the Christ. Early in the Book of Mormon account we read Nephi's statement that "six hundred years from the time that my father left Jerusalem, a prophet would the Lord God raise up among the Jews—even a Messiah, or, in other words, a Savior of the world" (1 Nephi 10:4). Nephi saw in vision that Jesus would be "lifted up upon the cross and slain for the sins of the world" (1 Nephi 11:33). Almost six hundred years before the birth of Jesus in Bethlehem, Lehi taught his son Jacob that "redemption cometh in and through the Holy Messiah; for he is full of grace and truth." Further, he explained, "there is no flesh that can dwell in the presence of God, save it be through the merits, and mercy, and grace of the Holy Messiah, who layeth down his life according to the flesh, and taketh it again by the power of the Spirit, that he may bring to pass the resurrection of the dead, being the first that should rise" (2 Nephi 2:6, 8). Alma taught an erring son that because the souls of God's children who lived before the meridian of time are just as precious in the sight of their Father as those who lived during or after that age, it is necessary that redemption in Christ should be available to people of all ages (Alma 39:17–19). Indeed, "none of the prophets have written, nor prophesied, save they have spoken concerning this Christ" (Jacob 7:11; compare 4:4; Mosiah 13:33).

ETERNAL COVENANTS AND ORDINANCES

Because we know that the great plan of happiness is eternal and that salvation in any age is accomplished only in and through the mediation of the Redeemer, we also know that the covenants and ordinances are likewise eternal and unchanging. "Now taking it for granted that the scriptures say what they mean, and mean what they say," the Prophet Joseph noted, "we have sufficient grounds to go on and prove from the Bible that the gospel has always been the same; the ordinances to fulfill its requirements, the same, and the officers to officiate, the same; and the signs and fruits resulting from the promises, the same." He continued with an illustration of this principle: "Therefore, as Noah was a preacher of righteousness he must have been baptized and ordained to the priesthood by the laying on of the hands."[3] In short, the Lord "set the ordinances to be the same forever and ever."[4] That is, "ordinances instituted in the heavens before the foundation of the world, in the priesthood, for the salvation of men, are not to be altered or changed. All must be saved on the same principles."[5]

It is in this light that we speak of the restored gospel as comprising the new and everlasting covenant. Modern revelations affirm: "Wherefore, I say unto you that I have sent unto you mine everlasting covenant, even that which was from the beginning" (D&C 49:9). "Verily I say unto you, blessed are you for receiving mine everlasting covenant, even the fulness of my gospel, sent forth unto the children of men, that they might have life and be made partakers of the glories which are to be revealed in the last days, as it was written by the prophets and apostles in days of old" (D&C 66:2; compare 1:22; 39:11; 45:9; 49:9; 133:57). President Joseph Fielding Smith declared, "The new and everlasting covenant is the sum total of all gospel covenants and obligations."[6] The gospel covenant is *new* in the sense that it was revealed anew following a period of apostasy. It is *everlasting* in the sense that it was had from the beginning.

Knowing what we do about the everlasting nature of the gospel, the Church and kingdom, and the principles and ordinances pertaining thereto, we recognize that many of the ancients had the gospel. Many of them knew the Lord, taught his doctrine, and officiated as legal administrators in his earthly kingdom. Abraham, Isaac, Jacob, Joseph, and all the other patriarchs enjoyed personal revelation and communion with their Maker. We would suppose that Eve and Sarah and Rebekah were baptized, that Jacob received the temple endowment, that Micah and Malachi stood in the prophetic office by divine call and not because they assumed that role on their own. Surely Nephi, son of Lehi, was baptized by water and received the gift of the Holy Ghost, as well as the high priesthood, although an account of his receiving those ordinances is not stated directly in the Nephite record. That the blessings of the holy temple were available to Former-day Saints is made clear in the Prophet's translation of the Egyptian papyri. We are told that one particular figure represents "the grand Key-words of the Holy Priesthood, as revealed to Adam, in the Garden of Eden, as also to Seth, Noah, Melchizedek, Abraham, and all to whom the Priesthood was revealed" (Explanation of Figure 3 in Facsimile 2). Because of what has been made known through Joseph Smith— principles of doctrine and priesthood government—we know what it takes to operate the kingdom of God and what the people of God must do to comply.

OUR FATHER LOVES ALL HIS CHILDREN

Several years ago on a Sabbath day I sat with an associate in his beautiful cathedral and listened as the priest spoke of the body and blood of Jesus. Out of the corner of my eye I noticed tears making their way down the cheeks of my friend. My mind reviewed the years of our association, and memory impressed upon me the reality of my friend's commitment to his faith, his goodness as a human being, and his genuine, heartfelt desire to be true to what he understood. There came over me the quiet, compelling realization that the Almighty loves this man as much as he loves me; that he is a child of our Heavenly Father, just as I am; and that the Lord will do all that is possible to maximize this man's opportunities and ensure his ultimate happiness.

That was an important moment in my life. I grew up with a testimony. It has never been difficult for me to believe. Though I was reared in a part of the country where there were few members of the Church around me, I sensed deep in my bones that what we are about in The Church of Jesus Christ of Latter-day Saints is true, is right, and is meant for blessing the entire world. On that particular occasion, however, as my friend and I sat reverently in a place that was somewhat foreign to my spiritual upbringing, there grew within me an awareness that God loves all people of all ages and is no respecter of persons. I knew then, of course, as I know now, that this is the only true and living Church and that the Latter-day Saints are the custodians of the fulness of the gospel and the holy priesthood. There is no question whatsoever about that. But I perceived then—and as I grow older, I perceive even more clearly—the goodness and mercy and infinite patience of our Heavenly Father toward all his sons and daughters. As Enoch observed, "Thou art there, and thy bosom is there; and also thou art just; thou art merciful and kind forever" (Moses 7:30).

I had a similar experience not long after my visit to the

cathedral. I picked up a copy of *Reader's Digest,* only to discover an insert on how to communicate more effectively with family members. It was prepared by The Church of Jesus Christ of Latter-day Saints. I was aware that the Church had begun placing these brief advertisements in the *Digest* but had never done more than glance through them. I read this particular one carefully. It was nice, had some good pointers on communication, and seemed to be the kind of thing that would leave a positive impression with most readers. My next thought was rather judgmental: "This is quaint, but it really isn't going to bring many people into the Church. Why waste the Church's money on such a thing?"

Then came the simple but effective chastisement to my narrow mind. It occurred to me that there just might be someone, somewhere who would be prompted, after reading the insert, to inquire after the Church and its teachings. More important, maybe someone would be helped by the piece. Maybe some father or mother, some son or daughter, would take counsel and take heart from what was written. Such individuals might not join the Church, but what if the insert actually helped their family, resulted in greater harmony, moved home a little closer to heaven? Wouldn't that make it worthwhile? My views were broadened through that experience and my awareness increased that the God and Father of us all will give unto us line upon line, precept upon precept, according to our ability and willingness to receive.

"All That He Seeth Fit That They Should Have"

We have only to wrestle personally with the pain of a wandering child or other loved one, or share the pain of someone who does, to realize that we do not cease to love the straying or the ignorant. And surely he who is the embodiment of love and mercy does not cease to love those of his children who do not enjoy the fulness of gospel blessings in their lives. Our Father in Heaven will surely do all that is appropriate during our mortal probation to inspire, lift, edify, and encourage individuals, families, communities, and nations. It was to Nephi that the Lord Jehovah spoke on this matter: "Know ye not that there are more nations than one? Know ye not that I, the Lord your God, have created all men, and that I remember those who are upon the isles of the sea; and that I rule in the heavens above and in the earth beneath; and that *I bring forth my word unto the children of men, yea, even upon all the nations of the earth?* . . . For behold, I shall speak unto the Jews and they shall write it; and I shall also speak unto the Nephites and they shall write it; and I shall also speak unto the other tribes of the house of Israel, which I have led away, and they shall write it; *and I shall also speak unto all nations of the earth and they shall write it*" (2 Nephi 29:7, 12; emphasis added).

Alma explained that "the Lord doth grant unto all nations, of their own nation and tongue, to teach his word, yea, in wisdom, all that he seeth fit they should have" (Alma 29:8). One body of people may be prepared for the fulness of light and knowledge; another body may be prepared only for a glimmer of that ray of truth. God suits his blessings according to the present readiness of the children of men. Elder B. H. Roberts offered the following counsel on this principle: "While the Church of Jesus Christ of Latter-day Saints is established for the instruction of men; and is one of God's instrumentalities for making known the truth yet he is not limited to that institution for such purposes, neither in time nor place. God raises up wise men . . . of their own tongue and nationality, speaking to them through means that they can comprehend; not always giving a fulness of truth such as may be found in the fulness of the gospel of Jesus Christ; but always giving that measure of truth that the people are prepared to receive. 'Mormonism' holds, then, that all the great teachers are servants of God; among all nations and in all ages. They are inspired men, appointed to instruct God's children according to the conditions in the midst of which he finds them. . . . Wherever God finds a soul sufficiently enlightened and pure; one with whom his Spirit can communicate, lo! he makes of him a teacher of men. While the path of sensuality and darkness may be that which most men tread, a few . . . have been led along the upward path; a few in all countries and generations have been wisdom seekers, or seekers of God. They have been so because the Divine Word of Wisdom has looked upon them, choosing them for the knowledge and service of himself."⁷

It is but reasonable, therefore, that elements of truth, pieces of a much larger mosaic, should be found throughout the world in varying cultures and among diverse religious groups. Further, as the world has passed through phases of apostasy and restoration, relics of revealed doctrine remain, albeit perhaps in altered or even convoluted forms. Persons lacking spiritual insight and the faith that derives from a knowledge of Christ's eternal plan of salvation may tend to cast doubt on the true gospel, may point to legends and traditions of Creation epics or Flood stories that presumably pre-date the Pentateuch, may eagerly note similarities between ordinances of the temple and practices in pagan cultures, and may thereby suggest that Christianity has but copied from more ancient sources.

President Joseph F. Smith had much to say to those who seek to upstage Christianity. He taught that Jesus Christ, "being the fountain of truth, is no imitator. He taught the truth first; it was his before it was given to man." President Smith said further: "When I read books scattered . . . through the world, throwing discredit upon words and teachings and doctrines of the Lord Jesus Christ, saying that some of the ideas Jesus uttered, truths that he promulgated, have been enunciated before by the ancient philosophers among the heathen nations of the world, I want to tell you that there is not a heathen philosopher that ever lived in all the

world from the beginning, that had a truth or enunciated a principle of God's truth that did not receive it from the fountain head,
from God himself. . . .

"Let it be remembered that Christ was with the Father from the
beginning, that the gospel of truth and light existed from the beginning, and is from everlasting to everlasting. The Father, Son, and
Holy Ghost, as one God, are the fountain of truth. . . . If we find
truth in broken fragments through the ages, it may be set down as
an incontrovertible fact that it originated at the fountain, and was
given to philosophers, inventors, patriots, reformers, and prophets
by the inspiration of God. It came from him through his Son Jesus
Christ and the Holy Ghost, in the first place, and from no other
source. It is eternal.

" . . . Men are mere repeaters of what he has taught them. He
has voiced no thought originating with man. The teachings of Jesus
did not begin with his incarnation; for, like truth, he is eternal. He
inspired the ancients from the beginning, and when he came to
earth, he reiterated eternal, original truth, and added gloriously to
the revelations men had uttered. When he returned to the Father,
he still took, and does take, an interest in his children and people,
by revealing to them new truths, and by inspiring their actions;
and, as men grow in the knowledge of God, they shall become more
and more like him unto the perfect day, when his knowledge shall
cover the earth as the waters cover the deep."[8]

REMNANTS OF THE FAITH

Knowing what we know concerning God our Father—that he
is a personal being, that he has a body of flesh and bones as tangible as our own, that he is an exalted and glorified being, and that
this knowledge was had by many of the ancients—should we be
surprised to find legends and myths concerning gods who have
divine power but human attributes and passions? Knowing that

Adam and Seth and Enos and Cainan and Mahalaleel and others of the antedeluvians spoke of the coming of the Messiah and that the Messiah would come to earth as a man but be possessed of the powers of a God, is it not likely that they also knew that he would be born of a virgin? Should we be surprised to find pagan traditions of virgin births and divine humans?

Adam heard the divine voice saying, "I am God; I made the world, and *men before they were in the flesh*" (Moses 6:51; emphasis added). That is, men and women in the earliest ages knew of a first estate, a premortal existence. Therefore, is it any wonder that several religious traditions teach the idea of past lives? Inasmuch as the doctrines of rebirth, regeneration, resurrection, and the immortality of the soul were taught to Adam and his posterity, why should we flinch when we discover the misshapen doctrines of reincarnation, transmigration of souls, and rebirth in such traditions as Hinduism, Jainism, and Sikhism, or when we encounter a people such as the ancient Egyptians who were obsessed not with death but with life after death?

Of particular interest to Latter-day Saints is the resemblance between what goes on in our own temples and what transpires in sacred structures of other faiths. In many cases those resemblances may originate with earnest truth seekers who act without authority, even as did Pharaoh, great-grandson of Noah. Pharaoh, "being a righteous man, established his kingdom and judged his people wisely and justly all his days, seeking earnestly to imitate that order established by the fathers in the first generations, in the days of the first patriarchal reign, even in the reign of Adam, and also of Noah, his father" (Abraham 1:26).

Hugh Nibley spent a lifetime studying such parallels. He wrote: "Latter-day Saints believe that their temple ordinances are as old as the human race and represent a primordial revealed religion that has passed through alternate phases of apostasy and restoration which have left the world littered with the scattered fragments of the original structure, some more and some less recognizable, but all badly damaged and out of proper context. . . .

" . . . There are countless parallels, many of them very instructive, among the customs and religions of mankind, to what the Mormons do. But there is a world of difference between Ginzberg's *Legends of the Jews* and the book of Isaiah, or between the Infancy Gospels and the real Gospels, no matter how many points of contact one may detect between them. The LDS endowment was not built up of elements brought together by chance, custom, or long research; it is a single, perfectly consistent organic whole, conveying its message without the aid of rationalizing, spiritualizing, allegorizing, or moralizing interpretations.

"But what about the Egyptian rites? What are they to us? They are a parody, an imitation, but as such not to be despised. For all the great age and consistency of their rites and teachings, which certainly command respect, the Egyptians did not have the real thing, and they knew it. . . .

"The Mormon endowment . . . is frankly a model, a presentation in figurative terms. As such it is flexible and adjustable; for example, it may be presented in more languages than one and in more than one medium of communication. But since it does not attempt to be a picture of reality, but only a model or analog to show how things work, setting forth the pattern of man's life on earth with its fundamental whys and wherefores, it does not need to be changed or adapted greatly through the years; it is a remarkably stable model, which makes its comparison with other forms and traditions, including the more ancient ones, quite valid and instructive."[9]

And what is true of sacred practices and beliefs throughout the ancient non-Christian world is also true in today's modern Christian world. We know there was a Great Apostasy following the deaths of the meridian apostles and that plain and precious truths and priesthood authority were lost. We know that God began the restoration of truths and powers through Joseph Smith and will continue to do so into and through the Millennium. But because Protestants or Catholics do not possess the authority to act in the name of God does not mean they have no truth or that any scriptural interpretation from them is automatically incorrect or corrupt. Elements of enlightenment, remnants of truth, and aspects of the faith of the Former-day Saints may be found in modern Christianity. The Lord loves his children, all of them, and he delights to "honor those who serve [him] in righteousness and in truth unto the end" (D&C 76:5).

CONCLUSION

Good people in the world, men and women who love God, are earnestly striving to be true to the standards of decency and integrity they have been taught. Indeed, everyone has access to some measure of light and truth from the Almighty. President Brigham Young declared that there has never been "a man or woman upon the face of the earth, from the days of Adam to this day, who has not been enlightened, instructed, and taught by the revelations of Jesus Christ."[10]

The prophets teach that if people will be true to the light within them—the Light of Christ—they will be led to the higher light of the Holy Ghost found in the covenant gospel, presumably either in this life or in the life to come. "And the Spirit giveth light to every man that cometh into the world; and the Spirit enlighteneth every man through the world, that hearkeneth to the voice of the Spirit."[11]

In fact, is it not possible that one reason so many parallels and resemblances exist between the fulness of the gospel and the various approximations of the full truth is that men and women are responding to "spirit memories" of the past, those things we once knew but now seem just out of conscious awareness? "All those salient truths," President Joseph F. Smith observed, "which come home so forcibly to the head and heart seem but the awakening of the memories of the spirit. Can we know anything here that we did not know before we came?"[12] Is this not why so many who join the Church recognize in the teachings of the missionaries things that they feel they have always known, things, interestingly enough, that are not necessarily to be found in their former religion? We generally refer to those who come into the Church as *converts,* implying that they turned from another belief to embrace the testimony of the Restoration. Although that happens, in most instances those who are baptized tell us, essentially, "Everything the missionaries told me I already believed!" In fact, that which we call a conversion is very often the *awakening* of a distant memory, an echo from the past. "People ask me why I left my old church," the convert says. "I tell them it was not a matter of leaving my old church as much as it was a matter of coming home."

Christ's gospel is eternal. It was delivered to earth's inhabitants in the beginning. It has been preached through the ages by Christian prophets who knew their Lord and sought to be true to divine covenants and ordinances. In The Church of Jesus Christ of Latter-day Saints we attend to sacred matters, matters that are ancient and eternal, matters that were discussed and foreordained from before the foundations of the world, matters that will prepare this earth to abide the coming of the King of kings. What the Latter-day Saints believe is what the Former-day Saints believed. The covenants we make and the ordinances we perform link us to the past and point us to a glorious future. God loves all his children and is eager to enlighten them in whatever ways he can. We rejoice in our Father and God, and we rejoice in the knowledge that we are all part of his royal family. Like Nephi of old, we glory in our Jesus, for he has redeemed our souls from hell (2 Nephi 33:6).

CHAPTER FIVE

THE INFINITE AND INTIMATE ATONEMENT

Joseph Smith stated that the fundamental principles of our religion are the testimonies of the apostles and prophets that Jesus Christ lived, suffered, died, and rose from the tomb.[1] These singular and magnificent truths—what we call the doctrine of Christ—are foundational to all we believe and do in the Church; all else, however supplementary, is secondary. Truly, nothing is more central to the faith of the Latter-day Saints than the verity that men and women are fallen creatures, desperately in need of pardoning mercy and divine enabling power. That tender mercy, that uplifting and ineffable enabling power, come to us through the atonement of the Lord Jesus Christ, an atonement that is both infinite in scope and intimate in nature. The cosmic Christ is also a personal Savior.

INFINITE IN SCOPE

The scriptures affirm that the Lord's atoning sacrifice is indeed infinite and eternal in scope. A universal fall necessitated a universal atonement. That atonement is broad and deep and expansive.

Consider the following ways in which we may rightfully speak of an infinite atonement.

The Atonement Is Timeless

No doctrine is more distinctive in the restored Church than the eternal nature of Christ's gospel, the concept that Christian prophets have taught Christian doctrines and administered Christian ordinances since the days of Adam. Adam and Eve were baptized, endowed with the Holy Spirit, and taught the gospel. They then taught their children the great plan of happiness. Likewise, Enoch held the priesthood, Noah was a presiding patriarch, and Abraham understood and taught the gospel of Jesus Christ (see Galatians 3:8). For the ancients, whether they lived in the Old World or the New, prophecy of the Messiah was as history: "Wherefore, the prophets, and the priests, and the teachers, did labor diligently, exhorting with all long-suffering the people to diligence; teaching the law of Moses, and the intent for which it was given; persuading them to look forward unto the Messiah, and believe in him to come as though he already was" (Jarom 1:11). Or, as Alma explained to Corianton: "Behold, you marvel why these things [the Atonement] should be known so long beforehand. Behold, I say unto you, is not a soul at this time as precious unto God as a soul will be at the time of his coming? Is it not as necessary that the plan of redemption should be made known unto this people as well as unto their children? Is it not as easy at this time for the Lord to send his angel to declare these glad tidings unto us as unto our children, or as after the time of his coming?" (Alma 39:17–19).

The Atonement Overcomes Death

Nothing is more universal than death. We are all born into this world, and we cannot escape it except through that phenomenon we know as death. Were there not some form of intercession, some action on the part of One greater than death, we would remain as spirits forever and would also become subject to the evil one forever (see 2 Nephi 9:7–9).

Jacob, the son of Lehi, declared: "Wherefore, it must needs be an infinite atonement—save it should be an infinite atonement this corruption [this mortal, corruptible body] could not put on incorruption [an immortal, glorified body]. Wherefore, the first judgment which came upon man [physical death] must needs have remained to an endless duration. And if so, this flesh must have laid down to rot and to crumble to its mother earth, to rise no more" (2 Nephi 9:7). If there had been no resurrection, no breaking of the bands of death, no release from the stranglehold of the grim reaper, we would be of all people most miserable. But thanks be to God, Christ "hath abolished death, and hath brought life and immortality to light through the gospel" (2 Timothy 1:10).

The Atonement Defies Mortal Law and Logic

C. S. Lewis wrote: "Among [the] Jews there suddenly turns up a man who goes about talking as if He was God. He claims to forgive sins. He says He has always existed. He says He is coming to judge the world at the end of time. . . .

" . . . Now unless the speaker is God, this is really so preposterous as to be comic. We can all understand how a man forgives offences against himself. You tread on my toes and I forgive you, you steal my money and I forgive you. But what should we make of a man, himself unrobbed and untrodden on, who announced that He forgave you for treading on other men's toes and stealing other men's money? . . . He told people that their sins were forgiven, and never waited to consult all the other people whom their sins had undoubtedly injured. He unhesitatingly behaved as if He was the party chiefly concerned, the person chiefly offended in all offences. This makes sense only if He really was the God whose laws were broken and whose love is wounded in every sin."[2]

Jesus did what no mortal man or woman could do. The touch of his hand and the unspeakable power of his mediation defies what you and I understand about justice and mercy and right and wrong and restitution and punishment. Note Amulek's words to the errant Zoramites: "It is expedient that there should be a great and last sacrifice; yea, not a sacrifice of man, neither of beast, neither of any manner of fowl; for it shall not be a human sacrifice; but it must be an infinite and eternal sacrifice. Now there is not any man that can sacrifice his own blood which will atone for the sins of another. Now, if a man murdereth, behold will our law, which is just, take the life of his brother? I say unto you, Nay. But the law requireth the life of him who hath murdered; therefore there can be nothing which is short of an infinite atonement which will suffice for the sins of the world" (Alma 34:10–12).

The Atonement Is Infinite and Eternal

Why was Jesus able to carry out the infinite and eternal Atonement? One might answer: "Because he volunteered to do so, to serve as the chief advocate and proponent of the Father's plan in our premortal existence." That answer is correct. Another might answer: "Because he was sinless. He never took a backward step or a moral detour. He therefore was not required to face the demands of justice for his own misdeeds." That answer is also correct. Our Lord testified of his divine Sonship to the Jews in the meridian of time: "Therefore doth my Father love me, because I lay down my life, that I might take it again. No man taketh it from me, but I lay it down of myself. I have power to lay it down, and I have power to take it again. This commandment have I received of my Father" (John 10:17–18).

From Mary—his mother, a mortal woman—Jesus inherited

mortality, including the capacity to die. From his Eternal Father, the Almighty Elohim, Jesus inherited immortality, the power to live forever. Thus Jesus was in a position to give his life, to determine when his mission and his ministry were finished, when the debt had been paid in full, when he had descended below all things. And it was Jesus, possessing the everlasting powers of the Father, who had the capacity to rise from the dead into glorified immortality. Helaman taught his sons Nephi and Lehi: "The Lord surely [shall] come to redeem his people, but . . . he [shall] not come to redeem them in their sins, but to redeem them from their sins. And he hath power given unto him from the Father to redeem them from their sins because of repentance" (Helaman 5:10–11). Amulek stated: "Therefore, it is expedient that there should be a great and last sacrifice, and then shall there be . . . a stop to the shedding of blood; then shall the law of Moses be fulfilled. . . . And behold, this is the whole meaning of the law, every whit pointing to that great and last sacrifice; and that great and last sacrifice will be the Son of God, yea, infinite and eternal" (Alma 34:13–14).

The Atonement is infinite and eternal because Jesus Christ is an infinite and eternal being.

The Savior Saves and Redeems All That He Creates

"And now, after the many testimonies which have been given of him," Joseph Smith and Sidney Rigdon affirmed, "this is the testimony, last of all, which we give of him: That he lives! For we saw him, even on the right hand of God; and we heard the voice bearing record that he is the Only Begotten of the Father—that by him, and through him, and of him, the worlds are and were created, and the inhabitants thereof are begotten sons and daughters unto God" (D&C 76:22–24).

In 1843 the Prophet Joseph rendered the vision of the glories

(D&C 76) in poetry, writing the following as a parallel to those verses:

> *And I heard a great voice, bearing record from heav'n,*
> *He's the Saviour, and only begotten of God—*
> *By him, of him, and through him, the worlds were all made,*
> *Even all that careen in the heavens so broad,*
>
> *Whose inhabitants, too, from the first to the last,*
> *Are sav'd by the very same Saviour of ours;*
> *And, of course, are begotten God's daughters and sons,*
> *By the very same truths, and the very same pow'rs.*[3]

As Moses learned, Jehovah created worlds without number, and many of those worlds have "passed away"—gone on through the cycle of premortality, mortality, and glorified immortality—by the word of God's power, that is, by and through the redemptive labors of Jesus Christ (Moses 1:35; see also vv. 32–34).

Elder Russell M. Nelson of the Quorum of the Twelve Apostles testified: "His [Christ's] Atonement is infinite—without an end. It was also infinite in that all humankind would be saved from never-ending death. It was infinite in terms of His immense suffering. It was infinite in time, putting an end to the preceding prototype of animal sacrifice. It was infinite in scope—it was to be done once for all. And the mercy of the Atonement extends not only to an infinite number of people, but also to an infinite number of worlds created by Him."[4]

INTIMATE IN NATURE

God's Infinity Does Not Preclude His Immediacy or His Intimacy

Part of Christ's majesty and omnipotence entails his tender ability to minister to us one by one. Although it is vital that we see our Master for who he is—the Lord God Omnipotent, the God of the ancients, the great I AM—to recognize the chasm between the finite and the infinite and thereby humble ourselves before him, we must also understand that Jesus is knowable, reachable, and approachable. He knows us. He knows our names. He knows our earthly obstacles. He knows how best to lift us and liberate our captive souls. C. S. Lewis wrote that God "has infinite attention to spare for each one of us. He does not have to deal with us in the mass. You are as much alone with Him as if you were the only being He had ever created. When Christ died, He died for you individually just as much as if you had been the only man in the world."[5]

Surely no one has come to that marvelous discovery more powerfully than did Enoch. Witnessing God's sorrow at the sins and pain of the world, particularly in the days of Noah, Enoch "said unto the Lord: How is it that thou canst weep, seeing thou art holy, and from all eternity to all eternity? And were it possible that man could number the particles of the earth, yea, millions of earths like this, it would not be a beginning to the number of thy creations; . . . and yet thou art there, and thy bosom is there; and also thou art just; thou art merciful and kind forever" (Moses 7:29–30).

In perhaps the greatest messianic prophecy of the Old Testament, Isaiah declared that "it pleased the Lord [the Father] to bruise him [the Son]; he hath put him to grief; when thou shalt make his soul an offering for sin he shall see his seed" (Isaiah 53:10; Mosiah 15:10). While I am sure it did not *please* our Heavenly Father, in the traditional sense of that word, to witness the excruciating pain and agony and alienation of his holy and wholly innocent Son in Gethsemane and on Golgotha, yet our Father was pleased that redemption had been wrought and the ransom paid. Truly, once Jesus had completed his atoning mission in mortality and had descended below all things, he gave up the ghost and his spirit passed into the postmortal spirit world. In paradise he was greeted by "an innumerable company of the spirits of the just" (D&C 138:12), the faithful Saints from the days of Adam, those who had accepted Christ's gospel and been born again into his kingdom. It was there, in other words, that the Savior saw his seed (see Mosiah 15:10–11).

Elder Merrill J. Bateman has suggested an even more intimate way in which the Suffering Servant "saw his seed." "For many years," Elder Bateman explained, "I thought of the Savior's experience in the Garden and on the cross as places where a large mass of sin was heaped upon Him. Through the words of Alma, Abinadi, Isaiah, and other prophets, however, my view has changed. Instead of an impersonal mass of sin, there was a long line of people, as Jesus felt 'our infirmities' (Hebrews 4:15), '[bore] our griefs, . . . carried our sorrows . . . [and] was bruised for our iniquities.' (Isaiah 53:4–5.)

"The Atonement was an intimate, personal experience in which Jesus came to know how to help each of us.

"The Pearl of Great Price teaches that Moses was shown all the inhabitants of the earth, which were 'numberless as the sand upon the sea shore.' (Moses 1:28.) If Moses beheld every soul, then it seems reasonable that the Creator of the universe has the power to become intimately acquainted with each of us. He learned about your weaknesses and mine. He experienced your pains and sufferings. He experienced mine. I testify that he knows us. He understands the way in which we deal with temptations. He knows our weaknesses. But more than that, more than just knowing us, He knows how to help us if we come to Him in faith."[6]

The Atonement Bridges the Chasm and Brings Us into Communion with God

The Arabic or Aramaic word translated as *atone* is *kafat,* which means to embrace. Said Lehi to his children, "The Lord hath redeemed my soul from hell; I have beheld his glory, and I am encircled about eternally in the arms of his love" (2 Nephi 1:15).

"Be faithful and diligent in keeping the commandments of God," a modern revelation counsels us, "and I will encircle thee in the arms of my love" (D&C 6:20). Further, "behold, and hearken, O ye elders of my church, saith the Lord your God, even Jesus Christ, your advocate, who knoweth the weakness of man and how to succor [run to and assist] them who are tempted" (D&C 62:1).

The Atonement was made not just so that our sins could be forgiven, as central and vital as that is. It also offers us hope and deliverance from feelings of inadequacy, fears, abuse or neglect, jealousy, and unintended mistakes. In what surely must be the most expansive and all-encompassing of all scriptural passages relative to the breadth and depth of the Atonement, Alma testified to the people of Gideon of the coming of the Messiah. Note how far we are into his declaration before sins or transgressions are even mentioned:

"And he shall go forth, suffering *pains* and *afflictions* and *temptations* of every kind; and this that the word might be fulfilled which saith he will take upon him the *pains* and the *sicknesses* of his people.

"And he will take upon him *death,* that he may loose the bands of death which bind his people; and he will take upon him their *infirmities,* that his bowels may be filled with mercy, according to the flesh, that he may know according to the flesh how to succor his people according to their infirmities.

"Now the Spirit knoweth all things; nevertheless the Son of God suffereth according to the flesh that he might take upon him the *sins* of his people, that he might blot out their *transgressions* according to the power of his deliverance" (Alma 7:11–13; emphasis added).

The Lord Has Suffered Everything We Will Ever Suffer

The Atoning One knows our sufferings intimately well because he suffered them before we did. "Can we, even in the depths of disease, tell [Christ] anything at all about suffering?" Elder Neal A. Maxwell inquired. "In ways we cannot comprehend, our sicknesses and infirmities were borne by Him even before they were borne by us. The very weight of our combined sins caused Him to descend below all. We have never been, nor will we be, in depths such as He has known. Thus His atonement made perfect His empathy and His mercy and His capacity to succor us, for which we can be everlastingly grateful as He tutors us in our trials. There was no ram in the thicket at Calvary to spare Him, this friend of Abraham and Isaac."[7]

More Than Anything Else, Jesus Christ Loves Us

The deeper the love, the deeper the suffering on behalf of a loved one. After quoting John 14:27, "Let not your heart be troubled, neither let it be afraid," Elder Jeffrey R. Holland said: "That may be one of the Savior's commandments that is, even in the hearts of otherwise faithful Latter-day Saints, almost universally disobeyed; and yet I wonder whether our resistance to this invitation could be any more grievous to the Lord's merciful heart. I can tell you this as a parent: as concerned as I would be if somewhere in their lives one of my children were seriously troubled or unhappy or disobedient, nevertheless I would be infinitely more devastated if I felt that at such a time that child could not trust me to help or thought his or her interest was unimportant to me or unsafe in my care. In that same spirit, I am convinced that none of us can appreciate how deeply it wounds the loving heart of the Savior of the world when He finds that His people do not feel confident in His care or secure in His hands or trust in His commandments.

"Just because God is God, just because Christ is Christ, they cannot do other than care for us and bless us and help us if we will but come unto them, approaching their throne of grace in meekness and lowliness of heart. They can't help but bless us. They have to. It is their nature. . . . When [the Savior] says, 'Come, follow me' (Luke 8:22), He means that He knows where the quicksand is and where the thorns are and the best way to handle the slippery slope near the summit of our personal mountains. He knows it all, and He knows the way. He is the way."[8]

Learning to surrender, to submit, to lay our burdens at the feet of the Savior—this is the lesson of a lifetime. It entails putting off the natural man within us that wants to take control and sacrificing the carnal man within us on the altar of God. Peter pleaded, "Humble yourselves therefore under the mighty hand of God, that he may exalt you in due time: Casting all your care upon him; for he careth for you" (1 Peter 5:6–7).

As we learn to cast our burden upon the Lord, we come to appreciate in a whole new way, not just that he loves us, for that is obvious, but that if we let him, he will do the caring, the fretting, the worrying for us. He will care *for us.* The mighty change of heart of which the scriptures speak "is the change from being confident about our own efforts to the state in which we despair of doing anything for ourselves and leave it to God.

" . . . The sense in which a Christian leaves it to God is that he puts all his trust in Christ: trusts that Christ will somehow share with him the perfect human obedience which He carried out from His birth to His crucifixion; that Christ will make the man more like Himself and, in a sense, make good his deficiencies. . . . And, in yet another sense, handing everything over to Christ does not, of course, mean that you stop trying. To trust Him means, of course, trying to do all that He says. There would be no sense in saying you trusted a person if you would not take his advice. Thus if you have really handed yourself over to Him, it must follow that you are trying to obey Him. But trying in a new way, a less worried way."[9]

CONCLUSION

President Gordon B. Hinckley declared: "I sense in a measure the meaning of His atonement. I cannot comprehend it all. It is so vast in its reach and yet so intimate in its effect that it defies comprehension. When all is said and done, when all of history is examined, when the deepest depths of the human mind have been explored, there is nothing so wonderful, so majestic, so tremendous as this act of grace when the Son of the Almighty, the prince of His Father's royal household, . . . gave His life in ignominy and pain so that all of the sons and daughters of God, of all generations of time, every one of whom must die, might walk again and live eternally."[10]

The Atonement of Jesus Christ reaches beyond human comprehension and stretches the mortal mind. It also touches the hearts of those simple in faith and soothes and settles those who trust humbly in their Redeemer. The Atonement extends beyond this world as it creates peace and joy in our own inner worlds. The Christ of the cosmos is at the same time the Savior of a single soul.

CHAPTER SIX

WHAT HAPPENED
TO THE CROSS?

"Now the Atonement of Christ is the most basic and fundamental doctrine of the gospel," Elder Bruce R. McConkie testified
at his last general conference of the Church, "and it is the least
understood of all our revealed truths.

"Many of us have a superficial knowledge and rely upon the
Lord and his goodness to see us through the trials and perils of life.

"But if we are to have faith like Enoch and Elijah we must
believe what they believed, know what they knew, and live as they
lived.

"May I invite you to join with me," he asked the Saints, "in
gaining a sound and sure knowledge of the Atonement.

"We must cast aside the philosophies of men and the wisdom
of the wise and hearken to that Spirit which is given us to guide us
into all truth.

"We must search the scriptures, accepting them as the mind
and will and voice of the Lord and the very power of God unto salvation."[1]

In short, we need to be clear and direct and consistent in how
we teach the doctrine of Christ, how we declare the gospel. I do not

suppose that Elder McConkie was suggesting that we will ever in this mortal life understand completely the mystery of mysteries—how Jesus of Nazareth could take upon himself the sins of all humanity and how it is that he could rise from the dead and have that literal bodily resurrection pass upon every person who enters mortality. Rather, it seems to me that Elder McConkie's plea and yearning invitation is for us to search the scriptures, ponder the revelations, and attune ourselves to the Infinite in order to better understand what we are meant to understand—namely, how salvation centers in and comes only through Christ; how our Lord's suffering in Gethsemane and on Golgotha work together perfectly to satisfy the demands of divine justice; and how you and I are to remember, focus upon, and appropriate into our personal beings the precious gift made available by an all-loving Deity. To borrow Elder Boyd K. Packer's thought, for you and me to spend most of our time in the classroom or in our homes discussing related but peripheral teachings (as true and important as they might be) without erecting the vital bridge to the Central Doctrine is to rob our students and ourselves of the transcendent outpouring that attends a Christ-centered and a Christ-directed presentation.

Whole books have been written on the Atonement, but I wish to focus here on one specific dimension of the Atonement—the divine link between the Garden and the Cross. I want to look back at our past, examine where we are now, and look to the future relative to how we teach the Savior's suffering and how we communicate with those within the Church as well as with interested (and sometimes critical) persons of other faiths who may question our commitment to Jesus Christ.

The Bible and the Cross

As we study the Gospels and then move through the next section—what Elder Jeffrey R. Holland has called "The Acts of the

Resurrected Christ Working through the Holy Spirit in the Lives and Ministries of His Ordained Apostles"[2]—we proceed into what is for me the most stimulating, perceptive, provocative, profound, and inspiring section of all biblical teachings, the epistles of the apostle Paul. These epistles contain a treasure of doctrinal data, specifically insight into such matters as the nature of fallen humanity and the desperate plight of unregenerate man; a variety of approaches to understanding the Atonement (satisfaction, substitution, ransom); the transforming power of the blood of Christ and the work of the Holy Spirit in renewing and resuscitating the spiritually stillborn; the doctrine of justification by faith and salvation by grace; and the abundant life enjoyed by those who have become new creatures, have been conformed to the image of the Savior and granted the mind of Christ.

Paul uses certain key words to denote a greater and grander and broader concept. For example, the word *circumcision* comes to convey much more than the rite performed on eight-day-old male children, a token of the covenant given to Father Abraham. Circumcision comes to denote Jewishness, Judaism, life under the law of Moses with the onerous expectations of obedience to the 613 commandments of Torah. Similarly, Paul's use of the word *cross* in reference to the crucifixion of Jesus comes to mean more than simply the mode of torture and execution invented by the Persians and perfected by the Romans. It was a sign, a token of the Atonement. To say that one believed in and taught the cross was to say that one accepted the reality of the lowly Nazarene's suffering and death as having divine redemptive power. But this was no message that tickled the ears of those to whom Paul bore witness. Indeed, it was scandalous.

For example, Paul reminds the Corinthian Saints that the risen Lord had sent him "to preach the gospel: not with wisdom of words, lest the cross of Christ should be made of none effect. For the preaching of the cross is to them that perish foolishness; but unto us which are saved it is the power of God. . . . For the Jews require a sign, and the Greeks seek after wisdom: but we preach Christ crucified, unto the Jews a stumbling block, and unto the Greeks foolishness" (1 Corinthians 1:17–18, 22–23).

Why would the Jews and the Greeks have been so put off by the idea of a crucified savior? For one thing, Moses had decreed that any person who was hanged on a tree is cursed by God (Deuteronomy 21:23). What, then, do we make of the outlandish claim that God had cursed the One who claimed to be God? That is, God had cursed himself! Ridiculous. In an irony of ironies, the One who had come into the world as the Tree of Life, the Tree of Blessing, hung and bled and suffered and died on the tree of cursing, the tree of death.

"From both the Greek and Roman points of view, the stigma of crucifixion made the whole notion of the gospel claiming Jesus as the Messiah an absolute absurdity," Evangelical pastor John MacArthur wrote. "A glance at the history of crucifixion in first-century Rome reveals what Paul's contemporaries thought about it. It was a horrific form of capital punishment, originating, most likely, in the Persian Empire, but other barbarians used it as well. The condemned died an agonizingly slow death by suffocation, gradually becoming too exhausted and traumatized to pull himself up on the nails in his hands, or push himself up on the nail through his feet, enough to take a deep breath of air. King Darius crucified three thousand Babylonians. Alexander the Great crucified two thousand from the city of Tyre. Alexander Janius crucified eight hundred Pharisees, while they watched soldiers slaughter their wives and children at their feet.

"This sealed the horror of the crucifixion in the Jewish mind. Romans came to power in Israel in 63 B.C. and used crucifixion extensively. Some writers say authorities crucified as many as thirty thousand people around that time. Titus Vespasian crucified so many Jews in A.D. 70 that the soldiers had no room for the crosses and not enough crosses for the bodies. It wasn't until 337, when Constantine abolished crucifixion, that it disappeared after a millennium of cruelty in the world."[3]

Martin Hengel pointed out that "to believe that . . . the mediator at creation and the redeemer of the world, had appeared in very recent times in out-of-the-way Galilee as a member of the obscure people of the Jews, and even worse, had died the death of a common criminal on the cross, could only be regarded as a sign of madness. The real gods of Greece and Rome could be distinguished from mortal men by the very fact that they were *immortal*—they had absolutely nothing in common with the cross as a sign of shame . . . and thus of the one who . . . was 'bound in the most ignominious fashion' and 'executed in a shameful way.'"[4] Nevertheless, when Paul came to the Corinthians he "came not with excellency of speech or of wisdom, declaring unto you the testimony of God. For I determined not to know any thing among you," he wrote, "save Jesus Christ and him crucified" (1 Corinthians 2:1–2).

Note Paul's use of the words *cross* and *crucify* in some of his epistles:

"Know ye not, that so many of us as were baptized [immersed, changed identity] into Jesus Christ were baptized into his death?

"Therefore we are buried with him by baptism into death: that like as Christ was raised up from the dead by the glory of the Father, even so we also should walk in newness of life.

"For if we have been planted together in the likeness of his death [that is, united with him in a death like his], we shall be also in the likeness of his resurrection:

"Knowing this, that our old man is crucified with him, that the body of sin might be destroyed [that is, rendered powerless], that henceforth we should not serve sin" (Romans 6:3–6).

"I am crucified with Christ: nevertheless I live: yet not I, but Christ liveth in me: and the life which I now live in the flesh I live by the faith of the Son of God, who loved me, and gave himself for me" (Galatians 2:20).

"For he is our peace, who hath made both [Jew and Gentile] one, and hath broken down the middle wall of partition between us;

"Having abolished in his flesh the enmity, even the law of commandments contained in ordinances; . . .

"And that he might reconcile both unto God in one body by the cross" (Ephesians 2:14–16).

"Brethren, be followers together of me, and mark them which walk so as ye have us for an ensample.

"(For many walk, of whom I have told you often, and now tell you even weeping, that they are the enemies of the cross of Christ . . .)" (Philippians 3:17–18).

"And [Christ] is the head of the body, the church: who is the beginning, the firstborn from the dead; that in all things he might have the preeminence.

"For it pleased the Father that in him should all fulness dwell;

"And, having made peace through the blood of his cross, by him to reconcile all things to himself; by him, I say, whether they be things in earth, or things in heaven" (Colossians 1:18–20).

"And ye are complete in [Christ], which is the head of all principality and power.

"And you, being dead in your sins . . . hath he quickened together with him, having forgiven you all trespasses;

"Blotting out the handwriting of ordinances that was against us, which was contrary to us"—that is, the Law pointed out the myriad of ways one could sin—"and took it out of the way, nailing it to his cross" (Colossians 2:10, 13–14).

Finally, let me point out one of my favorite New Testament

passages, one that is part of a verse in the beautiful hymn "When I Survey the Wondrous Cross": "But God forbid that I should glory, *save in the cross* of our Lord Jesus Christ" (Galatians 6:14; emphasis added). Clearly, the doctrine of the cross, meaning the doctrine of the Atonement, was right where it needed to be—at the heart and core of Paul's teachings. Neither the scandal of the cross—a word that was not even acceptable in polite Roman company—nor the absurdity of a dying Messiah could hinder the Apostle to the Gentiles from delivering his witness of the Christ to the ends of the known world. He was not ashamed of the gospel, which included Christ's sufferings and death on the cross (Romans 1:16).

We should note that historically, in the first few Christian centuries, the cross was not considered a virtuous or admirable symbol but rather a terrifying reminder of what Jesus and many thousands of others had ignominiously suffered. In fact, some scholars report that the cross did not appear in churches as a symbol of veneration until A.D. 431. Crosses on steeples did not appear until 586, and it was not until that sixth century that crucifixes were sanctioned by the Roman church.

LATTER-DAY SAINT SCRIPTURE AND THE CROSS

The Bible does not stand alone in testifying of the significance of the cross. Often I am asked why the Latter-day Saints do not believe in the saving efficacy of the cross, yet obviously we do. We proclaim, just as the apostle Paul did, "Jesus Christ, and him crucified" (1 Corinthians 2:2). It's just that our belief in the power of the cross is not well known among traditional Christians. For example, a woman in Canada asked my friend Pastor Greg Johnson how he could have close association with me and other Latter-day Saints.

"Why do you ask that?" he inquired.

She responded, "Mormons don't even believe that Jesus died on the cross."

Greg shook his head. "Where do you suppose the Latter-day Saints think Jesus died?"

"Oh, I don't mean that," she said. "I mean, they don't believe he died for our sins on the cross."

That is simply not true. Nephi foresaw the time, some six hundred years before, when Jesus would be *"lifted up upon the cross and slain for the sins of the world"* (1 Nephi 11:33; emphasis added). Much like Paul, Jacob called upon the followers of the Redeemer to experience for themselves the power of the cross: "Wherefore, we would to God that we could persuade all men not to rebel against God, to provoke him to anger, but that all men would believe in Christ, and *view his death, and suffer his cross* and bear the shame of the world" (Jacob 1:8; emphasis added; compare Moroni 9:25).

Notice the language of the risen Lord to the people of the Book of Mormon: "Behold, I have given unto you my gospel, and this is the gospel which I have given unto you—that I came into the world to do the will of my Father, because my Father sent me.

"And *my Father sent me that I might be lifted up upon the cross;* and after that I had been lifted up upon the cross, that I might draw all men unto me, that as I have been lifted up by men even so should men be lifted up by the Father, to stand before me, to be judged of their works, whether they be good or whether they be evil" (3 Nephi 27:13–14; emphasis added).

The testimony of the Doctrine and Covenants is that "Jesus was *crucified* by sinful men *for the sins of the world,* yea, for the remission of sins unto the contrite heart" (D&C 21:9; emphasis added). "I am Jesus Christ, the Son of God, who was crucified for the sins of the world, even as many as will believe on my name, that they may become the [children] of God, even one in me as I am one in the Father, as the Father is one in me, that we may be one" (D&C 35:2). In a brief passage on various spiritual gifts, a revelation in the Doctrine and Covenants affirms: "To some it is given by the Holy Ghost to know that Jesus Christ is the Son of God, and that *he was crucified for the sins of the world.* To others it is given to believe on their words, that they also might have eternal life if they continue faithful" (D&C 46:13–14; emphasis added). Elsewhere: "Behold, I, the Lord, who was crucified for the sins of the world, give unto you a commandment that you shall forsake the world" (D&C 53:2). President Joseph F. Smith was taught in his vision of the redemption of the dead that salvation has been "wrought through the sacrifice of the Son of God upon the cross" (D&C 138:35).

Scores of passages in the Book of Mormon and modern scripture speak of the vital need for Christ's suffering *and death.* That is to say, it was not just his suffering but also his death—on the cruel cross of Calvary—that was an indispensable element of the atoning sacrifice. Mormon explained: "Now Aaron began to open the scriptures unto them concerning the coming of Christ, and also concerning the resurrection of the dead, and that there could be no redemption for mankind save it were through the death and sufferings of Christ, and the atonement of his blood" (Alma 21:9; compare 22:14). In short, "he surely must die that salvation may come" (Helaman 14:15).

This doctrine was taught from the very beginning. Some three millennia before the coming of Jesus to earth, Enoch saw in vision "the day of the coming of the Son of Man, even in the flesh; and his soul rejoiced, saying: The Righteous is lifted up, and the Lamb is slain from the foundation of the world." Enoch looked "and beheld the Son of Man lifted up on the cross, after the manner of men" (Moses 7:47, 55).

We have no quarrel with those who speak reverently of the

cross, for so did those whose writings compose a significant part of the New Testament and those who spoke or wrote what is contained in our own scriptural records. The cross is a symbol. We are not opposed to symbols, for our people erect statues of the angel Moroni atop our most sacred edifices and wear CTR rings or other jewelry to point us to higher and greater realities.

Some wonder why we do not have crosses on our chuches. Although I am not aware of any doctrinal prohibition against the display of crosses, the historical fact is that many of the early Saints had Puritan roots. Puritans were opposed to excessive ceremony and ornamentation, including the use of crosses on their meetinghouses. In fact, early Baptists did not put crosses on their churches until they began to move into mainstream Protestantism sometime in the 1830s.

Although we as Latter-day Saints do not display crosses on our buildings, President Joseph F. Smith observed that "having been born anew, which is the putting away of the old man sin, and putting on of the man Christ Jesus, *we have become soldiers of the Cross,* having enlisted under the banner of Jehovah for time and for eternity."[5]

President Gordon B. Hinckley has said: "On Calvary He was the dying Jesus. From the tomb He emerged the Living Christ. The cross had been the bitter fruit of Judas's betrayal, the summary of Peter's denial. The empty tomb now became the testimony of His divinity, the assurance of eternal life, the answer to Job's unanswered question: 'If a man die, shall he live again?' (Job 14:14)."

THE GARDEN OF GETHSEMANE AND THE CROSS

"We, the Latter-day Saints, take the liberty of believing more than our Christian brethren: we not only believe . . . the Bible, but . . . the whole of the plan of salvation that Jesus has given to us. Do we differ from others who believe in the Lord Jesus Christ? No, only in believing more."[6] These words, uttered by President

Brigham Young, have come to mean more and more to me as I have worked closely with noble men and women of other Christian faiths. I have come to perceive that while there are significant doctrinal differences between us, a striking number of similarities emerges, once those involved in discussion are able to put away arrogance and pettiness and defensiveness, once the participants are more concerned with arriving at a deeper understanding of the truth than they are with proving the other to be wrongheaded.

Professor Douglas Davies of Durham University in England wrote: "Christians have paid relatively little attention to what befell Jesus in the Garden of Gethsemane compared with what happened to him at the Last Supper and on Calvary. This is as true for artists as it is for theologians. There are innumerable paintings of the Crucifixion but relatively few dealing with Christ's Passion in the garden. So, too, with theology: there is much written about the Eucharist and Christ's death but much less on his personal trial in the garden." Professor Davies describes the Master's anguish in Gethsemane as a betrayal of sorts, one instance among many during the long hours of atonement, in which Jesus was left alone, this time by the Father himself.[7]

In fact, one of the distinctive teachings of Mormonism is the central role of Gethsemane—that our Lord's suffering there was not simply an awful anticipation of Calvary but that it was redemptive in nature. Luke is the only Gospel writer who records that the Savior's agony in the Garden was of such magnitude that it caused him to sweat blood. This passage is disputed by some biblical scholars who identify it as of later origin and one that could have been used or omitted by those involved in the centuries-long controversy over the humanity/divinity of Jesus.[8] We know from King Benjamin (Mosiah 3:7) as well as from a revelation to Joseph Smith (D&C 19:18) that the sobering incident of the bloody sweat was historical, real, and meaningful. We know further from President

Brigham Young that the withdrawal of the Father's Spirit from his Son is what caused the only Perfect Being to bleed from every pore. That shedding of blood was a direct result of Jesus' becoming, in Paul's language, "sin for us" (2 Corinthians 5:21; compare Galatians 3:13) and thereby assuming the burden and effects of our temptations, sins, pains, afflictions, infirmities, and sicknesses.[9]

It is inevitable that over time individuals and whole faith communities begin to define themselves, at least to some extent, over against what others believe and thus to emphasize more strongly the doctrinal distinctions that make them who they are. So it was with the hours of atonement. Because we as Latter-day Saints have come to know, through the Book of Mormon and Doctrine and Covenants, concerning the purposes for the Master's pains in the Garden, we seem to have placed a greater emphasis upon Gethsemane than upon the cross. As time has passed, however, the leaders of the Church have begun to speak of the importance of both Gethsemane and the cross and to emphasize that what began in Gethsemane was completed on Golgotha. Note, for example, some of the following teachings of Church leaders:

From Elder John Taylor: "The plan, the arrangement, the agreement, the covenant was made, entered into, and accepted before the foundation of the world; it was prefigured by sacrifices, and was carried out and consummated on the cross."[10]

In June 1888 the General Superintendency of the Young Men's Mutual Improvement Association (Elders Wilford Woodruff, Joseph F. Smith, and Moses Thatcher) wrote: "Alone, while treading the wine-press of the wrath of devils and men, gained [Christ] the keys of death, hell and the grave. They were forged in the crucible of intense hate, not in the lap of luxurious ease. Ingratitude heaped upon Him the sins of the world, and heavy-eyed watchmen slept while He prayed and sweat great gouts of blood. Malice spat in His face; jealousy and mockery crowned Him with thorns; envy mantled Him with a cast-off robe; cruelty nailed Him to the cross, then cried: 'Come down, save thyself.' Son of God, Prince of Power, commander of heavenly legions though He was, the anguish of accumulated woes, caused Him, as death's agony bathed his brow, to exclaim: 'My God, my God, why hast thou forsaken me?'"[11]

From a Christmas epistle of the First Presidency (Heber J. Grant, Charles W. Penrose, and Anthony W. Ivins) on 17 December 1921: "We rejoice both in the occasion and in the opportunity; for we do know and do testify that He whose mortal birth in the Manger of Bethlehem the world celebrates at this festive season, is indeed the Son of God and the Savior of mankind through the atonement wrought out on the Cross of Calvary."[12]

President B. H. Roberts of the First Council of the Seventy: "If it be true, and it is, that men value things in proportion to what they cost, then how dear to them must be the Atonement, since it cost the Christ so much in suffering that he may be said to have been baptized by blood-sweat in Gethsemane, before he reached the climax of his passion, on Calvary."[13]

Presiding Bishop Joseph L. Wirthlin in 1952: "To take upon one the name of Jesus Christ, to me, means that we will accept the Son of God as the Redeemer of the World, that we will accept his plan of salvation and live it as he has commanded us, and then to remember the great sacrifice that he made upon Calvary's hill."[14]

Elder Bruce R. McConkie in 1985: Jesus "carried his own cross until he collapsed from the weight and pain and mounting agony of it all.

"Finally, on a hill called Calvary—again, it was outside Jerusalem's walls—while helpless disciples looked on and felt the agonies of near death in their own bodies, the Roman soldiers laid him upon the cross.

"With great mallets they drove spikes of iron through his feet and hands and wrists. Truly he was wounded for our transgressions and bruised for our iniquities.

"Then the cross was raised that all might see and gape and curse and deride. This they did, with evil venom, for three hours from 9:00 A.M. to noon.

"Then the heavens grew black. Darkness covered the land for the space of three hours. . . . There was a mighty storm, as though the very God of Nature was in agony.

"And truly he was, for *while he was hanging on the cross for another three hours,* from noon to 3:00 P.M., *all the infinite agonies and merciless pains of Gethsemane recurred.*

"And, finally, when the atoning agonies had taken their toll—when the victory had been won, when the Son of God had fulfilled the will of the Father in all things—then he said, 'It is finished' (John 19:30), and he voluntarily gave up the ghost."[15]

President Ezra Taft Benson: "In Gethsemane and on Calvary, He [Christ] worked out the infinite and eternal atonement. It was the greatest single act of love in recorded history. Thus He became our Redeemer."[16]

At a First Presidency Christmas devotional in 1996, President Gordon B. Hinckley stated that "we honor His birth. But without His death that birth would have been but one more birth. It was the redemption which He worked out in the Garden of Gethsemane and upon the cross of Calvary which made His gift immortal, universal, and everlasting."[17]

More recently, in 2005, President Gordon B. Hinckley observed that the way we live our lives—patterned after the only sinless being to walk the earth—is the great symbol of our Christianity. He went on to add that "no member of this Church must ever forget the terrible price paid by our Redeemer, who gave His life that all men might live—the agony of Gethsemane, the bitter mockery of His trial, the vicious crown of thorns tearing at His flesh, the blood cry of the mob before Pilate, the lonely burden of His heavy walk along the way to Calvary, the terrifying pain as great nails pierced His hands and feet. . . .

"We cannot forget that. We must never forget it, for here our Savior, our Redeemer, the Son of God, gave Himself, a vicarious sacrifice for each of us."[18]

"Do you have a testimony of the Savior of the world?" President Hinckley asked. "Do you know that He was the first Begotten of the Father? Do you know that actually He was the Only Begotten of the Father in the flesh? Do you know that He left His royal courts on high and came to earth, born under the humblest of circumstances? He walked the dusty roads of Palestine, and gave His life on the cross of Calvary for you and me."[19]

WE SING WHAT WE BELIEVE

Those who may still wonder what Latter-day Saints believe relative to Gethsemane and Golgotha may profitably undertake a fascinating study of the 1985 edition of the LDS hymnal. There are 341 hymns and anthems within this volume. In the "First Presidency Preface" are found these words:

"Inspirational music is an essential part of our church meetings. The hymns invite the Spirit of the Lord, create a feeling of reverence, unify us as members, and provide a way for us to offer praises to the Lord." Now note these words: *Some of the greatest sermons are preached by the singing of hymns.* Hymns move us to repentance and good works, build testimony and faith, comfort the weary, console the mourning, and inspire us to endure to the end." Later in the preface the Brethren add: "We hope the hymnbook will take a prominent place among the scriptures and other religious books in our homes."[20]

Many of the hymns were written by devoted Protestant or Catholic Christians, and a goodly number by Latter-day Saints.

All of them have been approved by the general leaders of the Church, the Church Music department, and the Correlation department. Scores of hymns give voice to our desire to submit and surrender to the Almighty, praise him for his goodness and grace, and petition for forgiveness, renewal, comfort, peace, strength, and eternal life. Of especial importance are the hymns sung prior to the administration of the sacrament, for they focus specifically on our Lord's suffering and death. For example, consider the inspiring words of the following (see also *Hymns,* nos. 171–73, 181, 190, 195):

> *As now we take the sacrament,*
> *Our thoughts are turned to thee,*
> *Thou Son of God, who lived for us,*
> *Then died on Calvary.*
> *We contemplate thy lasting grace,*
> *Thy boundless charity;*
> *To us the gift of life was giv'n*
> *For all eternity. (*Hymns, *no. 169)*

> *'Tis sweet to sing the matchless love*
> *Of Him who left his home above*
> *And came to earth—oh, wondrous plan—*
> *To suffer, bleed, and die for man.*

> *For Jesus died on Calvary,*
> *That all through him might ransomed be.*
> *Then sing hosannas to his name;*
> *Let heav'n and earth his love proclaim. (*Hymns, *no. 177)*

> *Rev'rently and meekly now,*
> *Let thy head most humbly bow.*
> *Think of me, thou ransomed one,*
> *Think what I for thee have done.*
> *With my blood that dripped like rain,*

Sweat in agony of pain,
With my body on the tree
I have ransomed even thee. (Hymns, *no. 185)*

Come, Saints, and drop a tear or two
For him who groaned beneath your load;
He shed a thousand drops for you,
A thousand drops of precious blood. (Hymns, *no. 192)*

I stand all amazed at the love Jesus offers me,
Confused at the grace that so fully he proffers me.
I tremble to know that for me he was crucified,
That for me, a sinner, he suffered, he bled and died.
    (Hymns, *no. 193)*

How great the wisdom and the love
That filled the courts on high
And sent the Savior from above
To suffer, bleed, and die!

How great, how glorious, how complete,
Redemption's grand design,
Where justice, love, and mercy meet
In harmony divine! (Hymns, *no. 195)*

Notice the repeated references in our sacred music to the Savior's suffering on the cross, as well as the occasional reference to his agony in the Garden. This helps to highlight the truth that we must tell the whole story of "redemption's grand design," to quote Eliza R. Snow. The hours of atonement—the hours wherein he who had come to earth in the name and by the authority of the Father to ransom fallen mortals and to open the gate to glorified immortality—were spent in incomprehensible agony, in awful alienation, in a struggle against the forces of death and hell, first among the olive trees and then on an accursed tree between two thieves. We cannot understate the price Jesus paid. We must not forget what the Messiah went through.

Conclusion

We know that no doctrine is more important than the doctrine of Christ—the good news, or glad tidings, that he came into the world to teach, testify, inspire, lift, heal, suffer, bleed, die, and rise from the tomb (see 3 Nephi 27:13–14; D&C 76:40–42). We must strive to teach these truths with passion, with plainness, with simplicity, and with consistency, knowing that only in this way will those who hear the word come to know to what Source they may look for a remission of their sins (2 Nephi 25:26). In this way, too, those outside our faith will come to appreciate more fully who we are and Whom we represent. They may not choose to join our church, but at least they will know that Latter-day Saint Christians have their souls stirred by the same message that fanned the flame in the bosoms of Former-day Saint Christians, even the message of mediation, the herald of hope, the declaration of deliverance. "As I grow in age and experience," Elder Boyd K. Packer stated, "I grow ever *less* concerned over whether others agree with us. I grow ever *more* concerned that they understand us."[21]

Yes, we do know something, something consummately precious about what went on in the Garden, something few people comprehend, and something we are under a mandate to declare as a part of the restored gospel. In addition, scripture and the prophetic word affirm the following from President Brigham Young: "I would say to my young friends . . . that if you go on a mission to preach the gospel with lightness and frivolity in your hearts . . . , and not *having your minds riveted—yes, I may say riveted—on the cross of Christ,* you will go and return in vain. . . . Let your minds be centered on your missions, and labor earnestly to bring souls to Christ."[22]

Our Heavenly Father "foreordained the fall of man," the Prophet Joseph declared, "but all merciful as He is, He foreordained at the same time, a plan of redemption for all mankind. I believe in the Divinity of Jesus Christ, and that He died for the sins of all men, who in Adam had fallen."[23] Such is the message of Mormonism, the foundation of saving faith, the fundamental principles of our religion.[24]

CHAPTER SEVEN

—·◈·—

THE GREATEST GIFT

We come unto Christ not alone to be taught but to be transformed. He is not only our Example but also our Change Agent and our Benefactor. Jesus is not just a convenient resource; he is the vital and indispensable element in our quest for happiness here and eternal reward hereafter. There is no hope and no possibility of reconciliation with the Father except by and through the Savior. The Atonement is that divine act of mercy and grace and condescension by which our Father and God opens the door to reunion with him. In and through Adam we partake of mortality and death. In and through Christ our Mediator and Intercessor, we partake of immortality and the abundant life. By means of the Atonement, the finite is reconciled to the Infinite, the incomplete to the Complete, the unfinished to the Finished, the imperfect to the Perfect. The Atonement, as an act of grace, demonstrates the love of the Father for his children. Jesus Christ, who lived a sinless and perfect life, claims of the Father "his rights of mercy which he hath upon the children of men" (Moroni 7:27).

CHANGE IN CHRIST

The Book of Mormon is a powerful invitation to come unto Christ and be changed. Indeed, one who chooses Christ chooses to be changed. The plan of salvation is not a program to make bad men good and good men better, though it certainly does that; rather, it is a system of salvation that seeks to renovate society and transform the whole of humankind. The Book of Mormon teaches that we are saved by merit, but not by our own merit. *"Since man had fallen,"* Aaron explained to the father of Lamoni, *"he could not merit anything of himself;* but the sufferings and death of Christ atone for their sins, through faith and repentance, and so forth" (Alma 22:14; emphasis added). This passage may require a bit of explanation. Of course we are expected to receive the ordinances of salvation, work faithfully in the kingdom, perform acts of Christian service, and endure faithfully to the end. Of course we are required to do the works of righteousness. They are *necessary* because they evidence our covenant with Christ to follow him and keep his commandments, but they are not *sufficient.*

Through the Church we receive the ordinances of salvation. Through the Church we sing and preach and rejoice. Through the Church we learn to love and serve one another, to contribute to the edification and growth of the "body of Christ," to officiate in a system of organized sacrifice. But our hope for salvation is not in a system, not in an organization, not in a program, inspired and God-ordained though they may be. Our hope is in Christ, the Person. In a world that offers flimsy and fleeting remedies for mortal despair, Jesus comes to us in our moments of need with a "more excellent hope" (Ether 12:32). What Jesus Christ *has* done speaks volumes concerning what he *can* do and what he *will* do for us.

Peace and strength here and salvation and eternal life hereafter come through the merits of Christ. Lehi explained to his son Jacob: "Wherefore, I know that thou art redeemed." Why was he redeemed? We know that he was faithful, as was his brother Nephi. We know that he saw the Lord, as did Nephi and Isaiah (2 Nephi 11:3). In short, Jacob was an obedient man, one who hearkened to the words of God and His servants. But that isn't why Jacob was redeemed. The full sentence reads: "Wherefore, I know that thou art redeemed, *because of the righteousness of thy Redeemer*" (2 Nephi 2:3; emphasis added). Jacob was bound for glory because of the goodness of Jesus!

Lehi went on to teach Jacob that "there is no flesh that can dwell in the presence of God, save it be through the merits, and mercy, and grace of the Holy Messiah" (2 Nephi 2:8). A converted Lamanite king exulted to his people "that [God] hath granted unto us that we might repent of these things, and also that he hath forgiven us of those our many sins and murders which we have committed, and *taken away the guilt from our hearts, through the merits of his Son*" (Alma 24:10; emphasis added). Samuel the Lamanite likewise called upon the sinful Nephites to believe on the name of Jesus Christ. "And if ye believe on his name ye will repent of all your sins, that thereby *ye may have a remission of them through his merits*" (Helaman 14:13; emphasis added). Truly, we go into the world and preach the message of salvation to our brothers and sisters "that they may believe the gospel and *rely upon the merits of Jesus Christ,* and be glorified through faith in his name, and that through their repentance they might be saved" (D&C 3:20; emphasis added).

Faith is the total trust, complete confidence in, and ready reliance upon the perfect merits, tender mercy, and endless grace of Jesus Christ for salvation. It is a gift of the Spirit (Moroni 10:11), a divine endowment that affirms to the human heart the identity and redemptive mission of the Savior. It is only through exercising faith in the name of Jesus Christ—meaning his power or authority, his atoning mission and work—that salvation comes to the children of men (Acts 4:12; 2 Nephi 9:24; Mosiah 3:17; 26:22; Alma 22:13; Helaman 14:13). In the words of Amulek, the atonement of Christ "bringeth about means unto men that they may have faith unto repentance" (Alma 34:15).

Elder Orson Pratt wrote that "the grace and faith by which man is saved, are the gifts of God, having been purchased by him not by his own works, but by the blood of Christ. Had not these gifts been purchased for man, all exertions on his part would have been entirely unavailing and fruitless. Whatever course man might have pursued, he could not have atoned for one sin; it required the sacrifice of a sinless and pure Being in order to purchase the gifts of faith, repentance, and salvation for fallen man. Grace, Faith, Repentance, and Salvation, when considered in their origin, are not of man, neither by his works; man did not devise, originate, nor adopt them; superior Beings in Celestial abodes, provided these gifts, and revealed the conditions to man by which he might become a partaker of them. Therefore all boasting on the part of man is excluded. He is saved by a plan which his works did not originate—a plan of heaven, and not of earth."[1]

In his enlightening and inimitable style, C. S. Lewis stated: "At first it is natural for a baby to take its mother's milk without knowing its mother. It is equally natural for us to see the man who helps us without seeing Christ behind him. But we must not remain babies. We must go on to recognise the real Giver. It is madness not to. Because, if we do not, we shall be relying on human beings. And that is going to let us down. The best of them will make mistakes; all of them will die. We must be thankful to all the people who have helped us, we must honour them and love them. But never, never pin your whole faith on any human being: not if he is the best and wisest in the whole world. There are lots of nice things you can do with sand; but do not try building a house on it."[2]

HIS ENABLING POWER

Without trust in the Lord, without recognizing our limits and learning to lean upon the merits of Christ, we will probably either work ourselves into a frenzy of spiritual and physical exhaustion or find ourselves doing all the right things but feeling little pleasure in doing so. Often we end up just going through the motions. There is a better and higher motivation, however, one that is above and beyond self-discipline, well beyond sheer will-power and dogged determination. It is a motivation born of the Spirit, one that comes to us as a result of a change of heart. Through the atonement of Christ we can do more than enjoy a change of behavior; we can have our *nature* changed.

"The Lord works from the inside out," President Ezra Taft Benson testified. "The world works from the outside in. The world would take people out of the slums. Christ takes the slums out of people, and then they take themselves out of the slums. The world would mold men by changing their environment. Christ changes men, who then change their environment. The world would shape human behavior, but Christ can change human nature." President Benson added: "Yes, Christ changes men, and changed men can change the world.

"Men changed for Christ will be captained by Christ. . . .

"Finally, men captained by Christ will be consumed in Christ."[3]

The grace of God is not just that final divine boost into celestial glory that a gracious Father and benevolent Savior provide at the time of judgment. We will, to be sure, require all the help we can get in order to be prepared to go where God and angels are and feel comfortable there; at the same time, grace is something we have access to every hour of every day of every year. "True grace," as Evangelical pastor John MacArthur explained, "is more than just a giant freebie, opening the door to heaven in the sweet by and by, but leaving us to wallow in sin in the bitter here and now.

Grace is God presently at work in our lives."[4] It is through the grace of God "that individuals, through faith in the atonement of Jesus Christ and repentance of their sins, *receive strength and assistance to do good works* that they otherwise would not be able to maintain if left to their own means. This grace is *an enabling power* that allows men and women to lay hold on eternal life and exaltation after they have expended their own best efforts" (LDS Bible Dictionary, 697).

The Lord provides for his followers a strength, an energy, a living power. It is by this means, by this new life in Christ, that we do what we cannot do on our own.

While serving as a priesthood leader many years ago, I had occasion to work with a young man who was struggling with same-sex attraction. He had violated his temple covenants but sincerely wanted to change. Church disciplinary measures were taken, and he and I began to work together toward change. He spoke often of how difficult it was for him to be active in the Church, to attend all the activities, and in general to be a typical Latter-day Saint when he felt so very atypical. He committed himself to avoid inappropriate sexual activity but wrestled with his same-sex attraction. One day he asked me, "If I do the things you have asked me to do—go to Church, read the scriptures, fast and pray, plead for divine help, receive priesthood blessings when necessary, and be chaste—can you assure me that the Lord will take away these desires, these attractions? Can you promise me they will go away?" It was a tough question.

As I recall, I said something like this: "I know that the Lord can indeed change you, change your heart, change your orientation. I know that he can do that instantaneously if he chooses to do so. I know that the power of change is in Jesus Christ and that dramatic and rapid change can take place. I do not know, however, whether the Lord will change you right away. I do know this, however: If you do what you have been asked to do, and if you do it regularly and consistently from now on, God will change you, either here or hereafter. You may be required to deal with these feelings until the day you die. But I can promise you two things—first, these feelings will eventually be transformed; and second, if God does not choose to bring about a major change in your nature in this life, he will strengthen and empower you to deal with the temptations you will face. You don't need to face this on your own."

I shared with my young friend a few scriptures that have special meaning to me. I reminded him that the celestial kingdom is the eternal abode of those who "overcome by faith" (D&C 76:53). I then turned to the Book of Mormon and read Alma's counsel to his faithful son Helaman: "Preach unto them repentance, and faith on the Lord Jesus Christ; teach them to humble themselves and to be meek and lowly in heart; teach them to *withstand every temptation of the devil, with their faith on the Lord Jesus Christ*" (Alma 37:33; emphasis added). Truly, Christ is our Advocate, the One who knows "the weakness of man and how to succor them who are tempted" (D&C 62:1). The devil doesn't need to get us to steal or lie or smoke or be immoral in any way—he merely needs to suggest that we understate, undersell, and underestimate the powers, appropriateness, and relevance of the gospel of Jesus Christ.

The Prince of Peace was sent to "bind up the brokenhearted, to proclaim liberty to the captives, and the opening of the prison to them that are bound" (Isaiah 61:1). Jesus Christ is the Great Physician, the One sent of the Father to heal our wounds, to dry our tears, to settle our souls. We live in a fallen world, a world of pain and trauma and tragedy, a world where bad things do indeed happen to good people. We live in a world where our goodwill is spurned, our noble desires are questioned, our benevolent deeds are rebutted. Life hurts. A lot. Sin on our part is only one way, albeit a significant way, by which we are wounded in mortality.

Very often others' sins against us result in pain and agony of soul. Abuse in its many ugly forms takes a terrible toll on human feelings of worth. Harshness, rudeness, callousness, and insensitivity—these are but a few ways by which Satan wins a battle through man's inhumanity to man. Each of us wrestles not only with sin and repentance but also with feelings of inadequacy, feelings of loneliness, bitterness, jealousy, or betrayal.

Alma explained that the Redeemer would "go forth, suffering pains and afflictions and temptations of every kind; and this that the word might be fulfilled which saith he will take upon him the pains and the sicknesses of his people.

"And he will take upon him death, that he may loose the bands of death which bind his people; and he will take upon him their infirmities, that his bowels may be filled with mercy, according to the flesh, that he may know according to the flesh how to succor his people according to their infirmities" (Alma 7:11–12).

This scripture points us to the Messiah's power to lift us, lighten our burdens, and cradle us amidst any care. It highlights the truth that Christ's empathy was made perfect through his participation in pain, our pain as well as his. Though Jehovah knew all things cognitively, there were some things he could only know experientially, some things he would be required to go through personally in order to be able to assist us, personally, in our passage through the second estate (Alma 7:13).

I have been inspired over the years in working with saintly persons who are seeking to recover from abuse, desertion, or betrayal. I have had reaffirmed, from witnessing their vexations of the soul, the eternal truth that mortals can do only so much in their feeble efforts to right the wrongs of this life. I have been deeply touched as I have beheld a miracle in process—their growing capacity to forgive. In our first meeting, there might have been much of bitterness and even of hatred expressed. As time passes, however, and as the Spirit of the Lord begins to work its marvelous wonders in the human heart, I have heard the offended one say such things as, "Well, I don't hate him [or her] any more. I don't want to be his closest friend, but I don't hate him. I can't." Then later I hear, "I am still troubled by what happened, but I no longer have bitter feelings toward this person." And then I hear: "I hope things work out for him. I deeply hope he can get his act together and straighten out. I want him to be happy." What a stunning illustration of a rebirth of the soul. Darkness and despair are replaced by light and peace. Doubt is replaced by confidence. Rancor is replaced by tenderness and magnanimity. Such a power, the power to take away the pain, turn away the anger, and put away the past—such a power is not of this earth.

We as mortals simply do not have the power to fix everything that is broken. Complete restitution, as we know it, may not be possible. President Boyd K. Packer explained that "sometimes you *cannot* give back what you have taken because you don't have it to give. If you have caused others to suffer unbearably—defiled someone's virtue, for example—it is not within your power to give it back. . . .

" . . . If you cannot undo what you have done, you are trapped. It is easy to understand how helpless and hopeless you then feel and why you might want to give up, just as Alma did.

"The thought that rescued Alma, when he acted upon it, is this: Restoring what you cannot restore, healing the wound you cannot heal, fixing that which you broke and you cannot fix is the very purpose of the atonement of Christ.

"When your desire is firm and you are willing to pay 'the uttermost farthing' [see Matthew 5:25–26], the law of restitution is suspended. Your obligation is transferred to the Lord. He will settle your accounts."[5]

This strength, this enlivening influence, this spiritual change, does not come to us just because we work harder or longer hours. It comes as a result of working smarter, working in conjunction with the Lord God Omnipotent. President Brigham Young likewise testified: "My faith is, when we have done all we can, then the Lord is under obligation, and will not disappoint the faithful; He will perform the rest."[6]

An Elusive Balance

The gospel of Jesus Christ is in fact a gospel covenant, a two-way promise. The Lord agrees to do for us what we could never do for ourselves—to forgive our sins, to lift our burdens, to renew our souls and re-create our nature, to raise us from the dead and qualify us for glory hereafter. At the same time, we promise to do what we *can* do: namely, exercise faith in Jesus Christ. Out of that faith will flow repentance, baptism and other ordinances, and faithful obedience. We know, without question, that the power to save us, to change us, to renew our souls, is in Christ. True faith, however, always manifests itself in *faithfulness*. "When faith springs up in the heart," President Brigham Young taught, "good works will follow, and good works will increase that pure faith within them."[7]

Latter-day Saints believe, with their Christian brothers and sisters, that salvation is a gift (D&C 6:13; 14:7), but we also emphasize that a gift must be received (D&C 88:33). One's receipt of the ordinances of salvation and one's efforts to keep the commandments are extensions and manifestations of true faith. In an effort to establish the appropriate balance, I have felt that it would be a worthwhile experience to list a few of the scriptural passages that affirm the need for works and that attest that individuals will be judged by God according to their works. This is certainly a key message in the Bible (see, for example, Psalm 62:11–12; Proverbs 24:12; Jeremiah 17:10; Matthew 7:21; 16:27; Acts 10:34–35;

Romans 2:6, 13; 2 Corinthians 5:10; Titus 3:8; James 1:22; 2:19–20, 26; 1 Peter 1:17; 1 John 3:18; Revelation 20:12).

The Book of Mormon: Another Testament of Jesus Christ has been given for the purpose of "proving to the world that the holy scriptures are true" (D&C 20:11). The following passages from that book of scripture affirm the vital place of good works:

"The day should come that they must be judged of their works, yea, even the works which were done by the temporal body in their days of probation" (1 Nephi 15:32).

"Yea, they are grasped with death, and hell; and death, and hell, and the devil, and all that have been seized therewith must stand before the throne of God, and be judged according to their works" (2 Nephi 28:23).

"And now I have spoken the words which the Lord God hath commanded me. And thus saith the Lord: They shall stand as a bright testimony against this people, at the judgment day; whereof they shall be judged, every man according to his works, whether they be good, or whether they be evil" (Mosiah 3:23–24).

"Do ye exercise faith in the redemption of him who created you? Do you look forward with an eye of faith, and view this mortal body raised in immortality, and this corruption raised in incorruption, to stand before God to be judged according to the deeds which have been done in the mortal body?" (Alma 5:15; compare Mosiah 16:10).

"Therefore, prepare ye the way of the Lord, for the time is at hand that all men shall reap a reward of their works, according to that which they have been—if they have been righteous they shall reap the salvation of their souls, according to the power and deliverance of Jesus Christ; and if they have been evil they shall reap the damnation of their souls, according to the power and captivation of the devil" (Alma 9:28).

"Therefore the wicked remain as though there had been no

redemption made, except it be the loosing of the bands of death; for behold, the day cometh that all shall rise from the dead and stand before God, and be judged according to their works" (Alma 11:41; see also 12:12).

"He [Jesus] shall rise again from the dead, which shall bring to pass the resurrection, that all men shall stand before him, to be judged at the last and judgment day, according to their works" (Alma 33:22; see also 36:15).

"And it is requisite with the justice of God that men should be judged according to their works; and if their works were good in this life, and the desires of their hearts were good, that they should also, at the last day, be restored unto that which is good" (Alma 41:3).

"Whosoever will come may come and partake of the waters of life freely; and whosoever will not come the same is not compelled to come; but in the last day it shall be restored unto him according to his deeds" (Alma 42:27).

" . . . the great and last day, when all people, and all kindreds, and all nations and tongues shall stand before God, to be judged of their works, whether they be good or whether they be evil" (3 Nephi 26:4).

"And for this cause I write unto you, that ye may know that ye must all stand before the judgment-seat of Christ, yea, every soul who belongs to the whole human family of Adam; and ye must stand to be judged of your works, whether they be good or evil" (Mormon 3:20).

On the one hand, Latter-day Saint scripture and prophetic teachings establish the essential truth that salvation is free and that it comes by grace, through God's unmerited favor. On the other hand, ancient and modern prophets set forth the equally vital point that works are a necessary, though insufficient, condition for salvation. We will be judged according to our works, not according to the merits of our works but to the extent that our works manifest to God who and what we have *become.*

C. S. Lewis explained: "Christians have often disputed as to whether what leads the Christian home is good actions, or Faith in Christ. . . . You see, we are now trying to understand, and to separate into water-tight compartments, what exactly God does and what man does when God and man are working together."[8]

What does it mean, therefore, to "work out our own salvation"? (Philippians 2:12). Certainly it does not mean to attempt to do it by ourselves, for the divine word is sure and clear: Such is impossible. Certainly it does not mean to accept Christ and his gospel and then live however we choose, utterly disregarding the standards of Christian discipleship. Such is an offense to God, and we will answer for the same on the day of judgment. No, it means to pray and trust in the Lord God as though everything depended upon him and also to work and labor as though everything depended upon him! If I rely *wholly* upon the merits of Christ (2 Nephi 31:19), how much do I rely upon myself to be saved? If I rely *alone* upon the merits of Christ (Moroni 6:4), how much do I rely upon myself to be saved?

The answer to both questions is a resounding "None." This is not a matter of self-confidence; it is a matter of confidence in Christ. I have a role in my own salvation, but peace and assurance and hope come because of what Jesus the Redeemer has done and will do to qualify me for life with him one day. Thus the grace of God, provided through the intercession of the Savior, is free yet expensive; it is costly grace, "costly because it costs a man his life, and it is grace because it gives a man the only true life. . . . Above all, it is *costly* because it cost God the life of his Son . . . and what has cost God much cannot be cheap for us. Above all, it is *grace* because God did not reckon his Son too dear a price to pay for our life, but delivered him up for us."[9]

Among the final words of Moroni on the last page of the Book of Mormon are these: "Yea, come unto Christ, and be perfected in him, and deny yourselves of all ungodliness; and *if ye shall deny yourselves of all ungodliness, and love God with all your might, mind, and strength, then is his grace sufficient for you*" (Moroni 10:32; emphasis added). For us to enjoy the strength, enabling power, and purifying influence of the mighty arm of God, we must do all in our power to receive it. Thus we reach and stretch to take the hand of the Almighty. We open our hands and our hearts to the proffered gift. We strive with all our souls to love our Maker and avoid those unholy attitudes and behaviors and places and influences that distance us from the Holy One. Then his grace is sufficient for us.

In a word, I am incomplete, or partial, while Christ is whole, or complete. As I come unto Christ by covenant, we (Christ and I) are complete. I am unfinished; Christ is finished. Through relying alone upon the merits of "the author and finisher of [my] faith" (Hebrews 12:2; compare Moroni 6:4), I become finished or fully formed. I am oh so imperfect; Christ is perfect. Together we are perfect. Those who come unto Christ become perfect *in him* (Moroni 10:32). Those who inherit the celestial kingdom are just men and just women who have been "*made perfect through Jesus the mediator of the new covenant, who wrought out this perfect atone-ment through the shedding of his own blood*" (D&C 76:69; emphasis added).

Because we are human—because we are weak and mortal and tired—we will probably never reach the point in this life when we have done "all we can do." Too many of us misread 2 Nephi 25:23 and conclude that the Lord can assist us only *after,* meaning following the time that, we have done "all we can do." In truth, the Lord can and does help us all along the way. I think Nephi is trying to emphasize that no matter how much we do, it simply will not be enough to guarantee salvation without Christ's intervention. Restating Nephi, above and beyond all we can do, notwithstanding all we can do, in spite of all we can do, it is by the grace of Christ that we are saved. And what is true of our ultimate salvation is true of our daily walk and talk, of our personality and our passions.

There is yet another way to look at 2 Nephi 25:23. Consider the conversion of thousands of Lamanites by the sons of Mosiah. The brother of Lamoni, named Anti-Nephi-Lehi, counseled with his people, who had made a covenant not to take up weapons against their brethren in war: "And I also thank my God, yea, my great God, that he hath granted unto us that we might repent of these things, and also that he hath forgiven us of those our many sins and murders which we have committed, and taken away the guilt from our hearts, through the merits of his Son.

"And now behold, my brethren, since it has been *all that we could do*, (as we were the most lost of all mankind) *to repent of all our sins* and the many murders which we have committed, and to get God to take them away from our hearts, for *it was all we could do to repent sufficiently before God that he would take away our stain—*

"Now, my best beloved brethren, since God hath taken away our stains, and our swords have become bright, then let us stain our swords no more with the blood of our brethren" (Alma 24:10–12; emphasis added).

There is a very real sense in which "all we can do" is come before the Lord in reverent humility, confess our weakness, and plead for his forgiveness, for his mercy and grace. It occurred to me recently that life is repentance, that progression and improvement and growth and maturity and refinement are all forms of repentance, and that the God-fearing live in a state of constant repentance.

The gospel of Jesus Christ is intended to liberate us, to lift and lighten our burdens. If it is not doing that in our individual lives, then perhaps our approach and understanding, our orientation—not necessarily the quantity of work to be done—may need some adjustment. Balance. *Balance.* That is the key. I have come to sense the need to balance a type of "divine discontent"—a healthy longing to improve—with what Nephi called a "perfect brightness of hope" (2 Nephi 31:20)—the Spirit-given assurance that in and through Jesus Christ we are going to make it.

CONCLUSION

I know of the power that is in Christ, power both to create the worlds and divide the seas and also to still the storms of the human heart, to right life's wrongs, to ease and eventually even remove the pain of scarred and beaten souls. There is no bitterness, no anger, no fear, no jealousy, no feelings of inadequacy that cannot be healed by the Great Physician. He is the Balm of Gilead. He is the One sent by the Father to "bind up the brokenhearted, to proclaim liberty to the captives, and the opening of the prison to them that are bound" (Isaiah 61:1). True followers of Christ learn to trust in him more, in the arm of flesh less. They learn to rely on him more, on man-made solutions less. They learn to surrender their burdens to him more fully. They learn to work to their limits and then be willing to seek that grace, or enabling power, that will make up the difference, for that sacred power makes all the difference.

As Moroni has instructed us, when we come unto Christ and seek to deny ourselves of ungodliness and give ourselves without let or hindrance to God, "then is his grace sufficient for you, that by his grace ye may be perfect in Christ"—whole, complete, fully formed; "and if by the grace of God ye are perfect in Christ, ye can in nowise deny the power of God" (Moroni 10:32). Those who completely surrender and submit to the Almighty cannot deny—block, stop, or prevent—the power of God from coming into their lives.

CHAPTER EIGHT

BEYOND THE VEIL

Knowledge concerning life beyond the grave came to Joseph Smith very early in his ministry. God the Eternal Father and his Son Jesus Christ appeared to the boy prophet in a sacred grove in the spring of 1820. In the midst of a light that shone above the brightness of the sun stood two holy personages, whose very presence attested to the reality of the life beyond. Subsequent appearances of holy messengers—sent to bestow knowledge, keys, and powers—would further testify that death is not the end.

"All men know they must die," Joseph Smith explained to the Latter-day Saints in Nauvoo, "and it is important that we should understand the reasons and causes of our exposure to the vicissitudes of life and of death, and the designs and purposes of God in our coming into the world, our sufferings here, and our departure hence. . . . It is but reasonable to suppose that God would reveal something in reference to the matter, and it is a subject we ought to study more than any other. We ought to study it day and night, for the world is ignorant in reference to their true condition and relation. If we have any claim on our Heavenly Father for anything, it is for knowledge on this important subject."[1] As a part of the

Restoration, the God of heaven chose to make known, line upon line, precept upon precept, the soul-warming verities associated with the third phase of our eternal journey we know as the post-mortal existence.

The Meaning of Death

Nothing is more common to mortals than death; death is the common lot of all who come into this life. Every person is born, and every person must die. All are born as helpless infants, and all depart this sphere equally helpless in the face of death. Death is something most of us fear, something from which we hide, some-thing most of us would choose to avoid if we could. Even among those who read by the lamp of gospel understanding, death is frequently viewed with fear and trembling. Elder Wilford Woodruff "referred to a saying of Joseph Smith, which he heard him utter (like this), That if the people knew what was behind the veil, they would try by every means to . . . get there. But *the Lord in his wisdom had implanted the fear of death in every person that they might cling to life and thus accomplish the designs of their Creator.*"[2]

In the purest sense, there is no death and there are no dead. When things die, they do not cease to be; they merely cease to be in this world. Life goes on. Death is a transition, a change in assignment, a transfer to another realm. When we die, the spirit continues to see and act and feel and associate; it is only the physical body that becomes inactive and lifeless for a season. And so we use the term *death* to describe what appears to be from our limited perspective. From an eternal vantage point, however, there is only life. We speak often of a person's "untimely death." Generally we mean that it is untimely for us, for those who remain behind. Though it is true that individuals may hasten their death and thus shorten their day of probation, for the faithful there is nothing untimely about death. President Joseph Fielding Smith thus stated:

"May I say for the consolation of those who mourn, and for the comfort and guidance of all of us, that no righteous man is ever taken before his time. In the case of the faithful saints, they are simply transferred to other fields of labor. The Lord's work goes on in this life, in the world of spirits, and in the kingdoms of glory where men go after their resurrection."[3]

In a sense, we die as to premortality in order to be born into mortality. Likewise, we must die as pertaining to time in order to be born into eternity. The separation of the physical body and the eternal spirit is a necessary part of the plan of God, for, as Alma explained, to reclaim man from this temporal death would destroy the great plan of happiness (Alma 42:8). Truly, death passes upon all humankind to fulfill "the merciful plan of the great Creator" (2 Nephi 9:6). It is merciful in the sense that it delivers us from the toils and agonies of this life. "When men are prepared," the Prophet observed, "they are better off to go hence."[4] In speaking of little children who depart this life before they arrive at the age of accountability, he said: "The Lord takes many away even in infancy, that they may escape the envy of man, and the sorrows and evils of this present world; they were too pure, too lovely, to live on earth; therefore, if rightly considered, instead of mourning we have reason to rejoice as they are delivered from evil, and we shall soon have them again."[5]

Death is merciful too because it opens us to a new phase of life, a time wherein the restrictions of this mortal body are gone and the mind or spirit can soar. Brigham Young, in speaking of the glory of what lies ahead, remarked: "I can say with regard to parting with our friends, and going ourselves, that I have been near enough to understand eternity so that I have had to exercise a great deal more faith to desire to live than I ever exercised in my whole life to live. The brightness and glory of the next apartment is inexpressible. It is not encumbered . . . so that when we advance in years we have to be stubbing along and to be careful lest we fall down. We see our youth, even, frequently stubbing their toes and falling down. But yonder, how different! They move with ease and like lightning."[6]

"How do we know," asked Elder Orson Pratt, "when this spirit is freed from this mortal tabernacle, but that all [our] senses will be greatly enlarged? . . . Unclothe the spirit, and instead of exposing a small portion of it about the size of a pea to the action of the rays of light, the whole of it would be exposed. I think we could then see in different directions at once. . . .

"I believe we shall be freed, in the next world, in a great measure, from these narrow, contracted methods of thinking. Instead of thinking in one channel, and following up one certain course of reasoning to find a certain truth, knowledge will rush in from all quarters . . . , informing the spirit, and giving understanding concerning ten thousand things at the same time; and the mind will be capable of receiving and retaining all."[7]

The severance of family ties through death is of all things most painful, bringing with it an avalanche of emotions, including loneliness and sorrow. Those of the household of faith are not spared such feelings. He who knows all things and has a present view of all time and eternity, even he is aware of such agonies. The Lord has said, "Thou shalt live together in love, insomuch that thou shalt weep for the loss of them that die" (D&C 42:45). We weep and we long for a reassociation, but we do not grieve in the same way as do those who have no hope (1 Thessalonians 4:13), for to do so is to express a lack of faith in the purposes of God and to ignore the promise of reunion and restoration given by our Lord and Savior. Indeed, life's bitter winters may find us walking alone. During these cold and dark seasons of solitude, we wrap ourselves in the protective clothing of faith and its perspective and are warmed by precious memories. Thus we move on, seeking always to view things as God views them. "Precious in the sight of the Lord," the revealed word declares, "is the death of his saints" (Psalm 116:15). We have the assurance from modern revelation that "those that die shall rest from all their labors, and their works shall follow them; and they shall receive a crown in the mansions of my Father, which I have prepared for them" (D&C 59:2).

Ten thousand times ten thousand things testify that death is not the end but rather a significant point along the infinite line of life. Truly, "this life is not all; the voice of *reason*, the language of *inspiration*, and the Spirit of the living God, our Creator, teaches us, as we hold the record of truth in our hands, that this is not the case, that this is not so; for, the heavens declare the glory of a God, and the firmament showeth His handiwork."[8]

We are born, we die, we are born again, and we die. And thus the cycle of life continues everlastingly. If there were no death, there would be no life. If there were no death, then the growth and development and expansion that lie ahead would be forever withheld from us. There is purpose in life, and there is purpose in death. He who knows all things orchestrates the events of our existence and knows what is best for us. The Prophet Joseph thus declared, "With respect to the deaths in Zion, we feel to mourn with those that mourn, but remember that the God of all the earth will do right."[9]

The Postmortal Spirit World

Modern revelation attests that the transition from time into eternity is immediate. As the individual breathes his last breath, his spirit leaves the body and passes directly into the world of spirits. Joseph Smith taught: "The spirits of the just are exalted to a greater and more glorious work; hence they are blessed in their departure to the world of spirits. Enveloped in flaming fire, *they are not far from us,* and know and understand our thoughts, feelings, and motions, and are often pained therewith."[10]

"Is the spirit world here?" President Brigham Young asked. "It is not beyond the sun, but is on this earth that was organized for the people that have lived and that do and will live upon it."[11]

Elder Parley P. Pratt similarly explained that the spirit world "is here on the very planet where we were born."[12]

At the time of one's entrance into the spirit world, one experiences what President Joseph F. Smith called a "partial judgment."[13] The person goes either to paradise or to hell (see also 1 Nephi 15:29; 2 Nephi 9:12). Paradise is the abode of the faithful, a state of happiness, "a state of rest, a state of peace, where they shall rest from all their troubles and from all care, and sorrow" (Alma 40:12). Paradise is a place where spirits "expand in wisdom, where they have respite from all their troubles, and where care and sorrow do not annoy."[14] On the other hand, the spirits of the wicked "shall be cast out into outer darkness; there shall be weeping, and wailing, and gnashing of teeth, and this because of their own iniquity, being led captive by the will of the devil" (Alma 40:13).

Modern revelation also makes clear that the entire spirit world, not just that portion known as hell, or outer darkness, is in a sense a spirit prison. Though there are divisions of some kind between the righteous and the wicked, all of the spirits of men and women are in one world, just as they are in the flesh. In the postmortal spirit world, the disembodied long for deliverance, seek for relief from their present condition; they look upon the long absence of their spirits from their bodies as a bondage (D&C 45:17; 138:50; see also 138:15–18, 23). "When our spirits leave these bodies, will they be happy?" asked Elder Orson Pratt. "Not perfectly so," he asserted. "Why? Because the spirit is absent from the body; it cannot be perfectly happy while a part of the man is lying in the earth. . . . You will be happy, you will be at ease in paradise; but still you will be looking for a house where your spirit can enter and act as you did in former times."[15]

President Brigham Young asked: "Where are the spirits of the ungodly? They are in prison. Where are the spirits of the righteous, the Prophets, and the Apostles? They are in prison, brethren; that is where they are." He observed: "I know it is a startling idea to say that the Prophet and the persecutor of the Prophet, all go to prison together . . . , but *they have not got their bodies yet, consequently they are in prison.*"[16] The Choice Seer, Joseph Smith, summarized: "Hades, the Greek, or Sheol, the Hebrew, these two significations mean a world of spirits. Hades, Sheol, paradise, spirits in prison, are all one: it is a world of spirits."[17] Thus for the apostle Peter to declare that Jesus went, after his mortal death, to preach to the "spirits in prison" (1 Peter 3:19)—and knowing from modern scripture that the Master did not minister in person to the wicked (D&C 138:20–22, 29, 37)—we conclude that he preached to the spirits in prison in the sense that he preached the gospel in the spirit world. More specifically, "from among the righteous, he organized his forces and appointed messengers, clothed with power and authority, and commissioned them to go forth and carry the light of the gospel to them that were in darkness, even to all the spirits of men" (D&C 138:30).

Just as surely as there are variations among the godly in paradise, so also there must be differences among those in hell. There are the very wicked who, as Alma explained, are subject to confrontation, suffering, and sore repentance. There are others—good people, on the whole—who have not enjoyed the blessings of the fulness of the gospel because such were unavailable to them. These work and grow and learn and develop. Many of them open their hearts to the gospel message and are taught. Modern prophets have further clarified that once the gospel message is delivered and accepted by individuals in the spirit world, and once the appropriate ordinances have been performed by those in the flesh who act as proxy for the departed, "the Lord has administrators there to set them free."[18] That is, once a person has received the gospel and its saving ordinances, he or she is permitted to cross the gulf that separates hell from paradise and thereafter enjoy sweet association with the faithful (Luke 16:26; see also 1 Nephi 15:28–30).[19]

Peter taught that persons in the spirit world are presented the gospel and are expected to accept it on faith, just as they would have been expected to do in the flesh (1 Peter 4:6). We do not suppose, knowing the goodness and justice of our God, that it would be any easier to accept the gospel as a disembodied spirit than it would to accept it as a mortal. And yet there are factors that bear upon a person's capacity to see and feel and hear and receive the truth. Some of those factors bear upon all of us, and some of them are beyond our power to control. As we move closer to the great millennial day, wickedness will multiply. The index of moral pollution will rise, making it more and more difficult to remain unscathed and unwounded in the war against evil. "It is my conviction," Elder Boyd K. Packer testified, "that those wicked influences one day will be overruled."[20]

Surely in the postmortal spirit world, persons will have such burdens as abuse, neglect, false teachings, and improper traditions—all of which can deter one from embracing the truth—torn away as if they were a film. Then perhaps they will in that sphere, free from Lucifer's taunts, see as they are seen and know as they are known. President Wilford Woodruff stated: "I tell you when the prophets and apostles go to preach to those who are shut up in prison, thousands of them will there embrace the Gospel. They know more in that world than they do here."[21] President Lorenzo Snow, presumably speaking of the honest-hearted individuals who enter the spirit world, also pointed out: "Within the last few months thousands of persons in the spirit world have been placed in a condition that they may receive the word of God and be saved, through the ordinances that have been administered in these four temples in this Territory. A wonderful work is being accomplished in our temples in favor of the spirits in prison. I believe, strongly too, that *when the Gospel is preached to the spirits in prison, the success attending that preaching will be far greater than that attending the preaching of our Elders in this life.* I believe there will be very few indeed of those spirits who will not gladly receive the Gospel when it is carried to them. The circumstances there will be a thousand times more favorable. . . . *I believe there will be very few who will not receive the truth.* They will hear the voice of the Son of God; they will hear the voice of the Priesthood of the Son of God, and they will receive the truth and live."[22]

"In this space between death and the resurrection of the body, the two classes of souls remain, in happiness or in misery, until the time which is appointed of God that the dead shall come forth and be reunited both spirit and body."[23] And so the postmortal spirit world is an intermediate stop for all persons. It is a place of waiting, of repentance and suffering, of peace and rest, and of instruction and preparation. Those who receive and enjoy the blessings of the gospel (celestial) or at least who receive the testimony of Jesus (terrestrial) will come forth from the spirit world unto the first resurrection (see D&C 76:51, 74, 82). Those who continue to assert their own will and refuse the Savior's offer of enlightenment and renewal will remain in the spirit world until the thousand years are ended. Then in that second, or last, resurrection they shall come forth, either to a telestial glory or to a kingdom of no glory (as sons of perdition; see D&C 76; 88:24, 32).

RESURRECTION AND JUDGMENT

The apostle Paul taught that "if in this life only we have hope in Christ, we are of all men most miserable" (1 Corinthians 15:19).

That is to say, if Jesus' greatest accomplishments consisted of his kindness, his generosity, and his sage advice, then our hope for happiness hereafter is unfounded. Like Paul, the Book of Mormon prophet Jacob declared that if Christ did not rise from the dead (as it was prophesied he would do), then we shall one and all, at the time of death, be consigned to spiritual ruin and destruction; we will be forevermore subject to the father of lies.

Why? Because if Jesus did not have the power to rise from the dead and thus redeem the body from the grave, then he surely did not have the power to forgive sins and thereby redeem the spirit from hell (2 Nephi 9:7–9; compare 1 Corinthians 15:12–17). "If the resurrection from the dead be not an important point, or item in our faith," Joseph Smith explained, "we must confess that we know nothing about it; for if there be no resurrection from the dead, then Christ has not risen; and if Christ has not risen He was not the Son of God." On the other hand, "if He has risen from the dead the bands of the temporal death are broken that the grave has no victory. If then, the grave has no victory, those who keep the sayings of Jesus and obey His teachings have not only a promise of a resurrection from the dead, but an assurance of being admitted into His glorious kingdom."[24] Because Jesus Christ has risen from the dead, we too shall rise from the dead. Because he lives, we too shall live beyond the grave.

The resurrected body is a spiritual body, meaning that it is immortal, not subject to death (1 Corinthians 15:44; Alma 11:45; D&C 88:27). The scriptures promise that we will come forth from the grave with a resurrected body suited to the respective kingdom we shall inherit:

"They who are of a celestial spirit shall receive the same body which was a natural body; even ye shall receive your bodies, and your glory shall be that glory by which your bodies are quickened.

"Ye who are quickened by a portion of the celestial glory shall then receive of the same, even a fulness.

"And they who are quickened by a portion of the terrestrial glory shall then receive of the same, even a fulness.

"And also they who are quickened by a portion of the telestial glory shall then receive of the same, even a fulness.

"And they who remain [the sons of perdition] shall also be quickened; nevertheless, they shall return again to their own place, to enjoy that which they are willing to receive, because they were not willing to enjoy that which they might have received" (D&C 88:28–32).

The scriptures of the Restoration further clarify the nature of the resurrected body: "The soul [here, the spirit] shall be restored to the body," Alma explained, "and the body to the soul; yea, and every limb and joint shall be restored to its body; yea, even a hair of the head shall not be lost; but all things shall be restored to their proper and perfect frame" (Alma 40:23; see also 11:43). In speaking of the righteous who waited anxiously for the Savior's entrance into paradise, President Joseph F. Smith wrote: "Their sleeping dust was to be restored unto its perfect frame, bone to his bone, and the sinews and the flesh upon them, the spirit and the body to be united never again to be divided, that they might receive a fulness of joy" (D&C 138:17). Latter-day prophets have told us that the body comes forth from the grave as it is laid down, "whether old or young; there will not be 'added unto their stature one cubit,' neither taken from it; all will be raised by the power of God, having spirit in their bodies, and not blood."[25] We understand that physical deformities will not be a part of the resurrected body, for "deformity will be removed; defects will be eliminated, and men and women shall attain to the perfection of their spirits, to the perfection that God designed in the beginning."[26]

Finally, we have the comforting assurance that even though we

are refined, renewed, and perfected body and soul in the resurrection, we will maintain our individual identity. We will know
friends and loved ones in and after the resurrection, even as we
know them now. Though Christians at the time of Joseph Smith
(and many do today, as well) spoke of being caught up into the love
of Jesus and blending into his nature, the revelations of heaven
declare otherwise. In speaking of meeting a departed loved one in
the future, President Joseph F. Smith taught: "I expect to be able to
recognize her, just as I could recognize her tomorrow, if she were
living . . . , because her identity is fixed and indestructible, just as
fixed and indestructible as the identity of God the Father and Jesus
Christ the Son. They cannot be any other than themselves. They
cannot be changed; they are from everlasting to everlasting, eternally the same; so it will be with us. We will progress and develop
and grow in wisdom and understanding, but our identity can never
change."[29]

In the Book of Mormon, resurrection and eternal judgment are
companion doctrines, just as are the Fall and the Atonement. One
of the great acts of mercy and grace is that all who took a physical
body, including the sons of perdition, will be resurrected and thereafter brought to stand before God to be judged of their works. In a
sense, therefore, the Atonement overcomes spiritual death for all,
at least for the short season wherein everyone stands once again in
the divine presence. Jacob wrote: "And it shall come to pass that
when all men shall have passed from this first death unto life, insomuch as they have become immortal, they must appear before the
judgment-seat of the Holy One of Israel; and then cometh the judgment, and then must they be judged according to the holy judgment of God" (2 Nephi 9:15). Samuel the Lamanite also declared
that Jesus "surely must die that salvation may come; yea, it
behooveth him and becometh expedient that he dieth, to bring to
pass the resurrection of the dead, that thereby men may be brought

the goodness of God," C. S. Lewis pointed out, "we mean nowadays almost exclusively His lovingness; and in this we may be right. And by Love, in this context, most of us mean kindness—the desire to see others than the self happy; not happy in this way or in that, but just happy. What would really satisfy us would be a God who said of anything we happened to like doing, 'What does it matter so long as they are contented?' We want, in fact, not so much a Father in Heaven as a grandfather in heaven—a senile benevolence who, as they say, 'liked to see young people enjoying themselves,' and whose plan for the universe was simply that it might be truly said at the end of each day, 'a good time was had by all.'"[5]

Someone else observed: "Theism does not affirm that God is always 'nice' or pleasant or kindly. God's goodness is absolute purity, as much like the purity of a blast furnace . . . as it is like the indulgence of a sweet grandmother. God always does the right thing; God always wills what is best; God always thinks without error, incompleteness, or prejudice. Such a God may not always be likable, nor always comfortable. But such a God may well be worthy of worship."[6]

Through the instrumentality of a modern prophet, light and truth and understanding concerning the true nature of God have come to us. The God we have come to know is an exalted Man, a Man of Holiness (Moses 6:57), a divine being who indeed has all power, all knowledge, and who possesses every godly attribute in perfection. At the same time, through the clarifying lenses provided by the revelations of the Restoration, the Latter-day Saints are made acquainted with a God who is in reality our Heavenly Father, the Father of our spirits; who has a body of flesh and bones as tangible as man's (D&C 130:22); who feels tender regard for all his children and is, like his Beloved Son, "touched with the feeling of our infirmities" (Hebrews 4:15); and who has granted us moral agency, the capacity to choose what we will do with our lives. As Elder Kimball pointed out, agency is paramount. In fact, as we know, agency was one of the central issues in the war in heaven (Moses 4:3), a war, by the way, that is still under way. We also know, in a very personal way, of the reality of evil and of the truth that Lucifer is bent upon our destruction and the overthrow of the Father's plan. He does everything in his power to pervert and corrupt the right way and to entice us to use our agency unwisely.

There is something even more horrible to contemplate than the Holocaust, more unspeakable than millions of innocent people put to death by crazed dictators, more frightening than terrorists hijacking airplanes and murdering thousands. Consider this thought: What if there were no agency? What if people did not have the right to choose? What if Lucifer's amendatory proposals in the grand councils of heaven had been implemented? Agency, one of the greatest of all the gifts of a benevolent and generous God, comes at a price. Allowing us to choose automatically opens the door to improper, unwise, immoral, and evil choices and thus to abuse and human tragedy.

Philosopher Richard Swinburne wrote: "A God who gives humans such free will necessarily brings about the possibility, and puts outside his own control whether or not . . . evil occurs. It is not logically possible—that is, it would be self-contradictory to suppose—that God could give us such free will and yet ensure that we always use it in the right way. . . .

"A world in which agents can benefit each other but not do each other harm is one where they have very limited responsibility for each other. If my responsibility for you is limited to whether or not to give you a camcorder, but I cannot cause you pain, stunt your growth, or limit your education, then I do not have a great deal of responsibility for you. . . . A good God, like a good father, will delegate responsibility. In order to allow creatures a share in creation, he will allow them the choice of hurting and maiming, of frustrating the divine plan."[7]

Swinburne observes further: "I am fortunate if the natural possibility of my suffering if you choose to hurt me is the vehicle which makes your choice really matter. My vulnerability, my openness to suffering (which necessarily involves my actually suffering if you make the wrong choice), means that you are not just like a pilot in a simulator, where it does not matter if mistakes are made. That our choices matter tremendously, that we can make great differences to things for good or ill, is one of the greatest gifts a creator can give us. And if my suffering is the means by which he can give you that choice, I too am in this respect fortunate."[8]

Or, as Professor Stackhouse wrote: "Why doesn't God step in to save us, we might ask, even from ourselves? But let us consider what we are asking here. If God does so step in, such continual intervention has implications for human dignity, for the order of the world, and perhaps for the ultimate good of human life. Maybe, in fact, it is *best* that God *does not* intervene, and lets us both make choices and live with the consequences."[9]

Where is God when it hurts? He is in his heavens. He is aware. He knows. In ways that we cannot even comprehend, he knows. And he blesses and lifts and liberates and lightens the burdens of his children whenever he can. But he cannot remove us from the toils and tragedies and contradictions of life without robbing us of mortal experience. These things come with the turf. They are part of the test. So much depends upon how we choose to look upon what most consider to be the unfairness and the senseless nature of temporal trauma. So much depends upon what we understand about God our Father, about his plan of salvation, and about how vital it is for us to move ahead, even when our burdens or the burdens of others seem unbearable.

Although a measure of joy and happiness and a sense of overcoming can be ours in this life, the fulness of joy is reserved for the next estate, when spirit and body are reunited in the resurrection (D&C 93:33). "Wherefore, fear not even unto death," the Redeemer declared, "for in this world your joy is not full, but in me your joy is full" (D&C 101:36).

President Boyd K. Packer explained: "There are three parts to the plan. You are in the second or middle part, the one in which you will be tested by temptation, by trials, perhaps by tragedy. Understand that, and you will be better able to make sense of life and to resist the disease of doubt and despair and depression. . . . If you expect to find only ease and peace and bliss during Act II, you surely will be frustrated. You will understand little of what is going on and why it is permitted to be as they are. Remember this! The line 'And they all lived happily ever after' is never written into the second act. That line belongs in the third act when the mysteries are solved and everything is put right."[10]

Elder Neal A. Maxwell taught: "When we tear ourselves free from the entanglements of the world, are we promised a religion of repose or an Eden of ease? No! We are promised tears and trials and toil! But we are also promised final triumph, the mere contemplation of which tingles one's soul."[11]

We shouted for joy in that premortal day (Job 38:4, 7) because we knew that there were lasting lessons and everlasting principles to be learned on earth, things we could neither grasp nor experience in our first estate. We shouted for joy because we knew that there were relationships to be developed, feelings to be felt, tests to be passed. We shouted for joy—knowing full well the struggle through which we would be called upon to pass—because we knew that it was all worth it.

Lasting Lessons, Tender Tutorials

Every one of us will, at one time or another, face adversity, whether it be in the form of financial reversals, personal struggles, the loss of a loved one, or some other profound disappointment.

Adversity will come to us, one and all, whether we are prepared for it or not. Too often in tough times we yield ourselves to stress and distress, to despondency and discouragement, much more so than our forebears would have. Certainly life is more complex, the demands on our time are more intense, and the temptations of the devil are more sophisticated. At the same time, however, it seems to me that a mindset characteristic of our day opens us to despair. That mindset is one in which we assume, given all the pleasures and luxuries of our day and age, that all should be well with us, that we should be perpetually happy. Many of us have imbibed the jargon and the philosophy of our pop psychology world. The fact is, life can be tough. We are not guaranteed a stress-free existence, nor did the Lord promise us a mortal life void of challenge and difficulty.

We are living in a fallen world, one in which things break down, decay, atrophy, and die. We are living in a mortal existence. Yes, there is much in the world that is glorious and beautiful and uplifting and inspiring; many of the relationships we establish, for example, are elevating and enriching—they bring the deepest of joys into our lives. But we receive our joys alongside our sorrows. Both elements of the equation come with the turf, with earth life. And we knew this before we came.

C. S. Lewis once observed that God "has paid us the intolerable compliment of loving us, in the deepest, most tragic, most inexorable sense." He continued, "We are, not metaphorically but in very truth, a Divine work of art, something that God is making, and therefore something with which He will not be satisfied until it has a certain character." Thus it is "natural for us to wish that God had designed for us a less glorious and less arduous destiny; but then we are wishing not for more love but for less."[12] "For whom the Lord loveth he chasteneth, and scourgeth every [child] whom he receiveth. . . . Now no chastening for the present seemeth to be joyous, but grievous: nevertheless afterward it yieldeth the peaceable fruit of righteousness unto them which are exercised [trained, disciplined] thereby" (Hebrews 12:6, 11). James, the brother of Jesus, instructed us to "count it all joy when ye fall into many afflictions; knowing this, that the trying of your faith worketh patience. But let patience have its perfect work, that ye may be perfect and entire, wanting nothing" (JST James 1:2–4).

In short, great lessons are to be learned from life's struggles, lessons that can perhaps be acquired in no other way. Many of our afflictions we bring upon ourselves through our own impatience, short-sightedness, or sins. I suppose lessons may be learned from our sins—not the least of which is the motivation to avoid in the future the pain associated with our misdeeds—but these are lessons I am persuaded the Lord can bring into our lives without our sinning. A man called as a bishop, for example, need not be troubled that he has lived a faithful life and thus may not be able to feel what the transgressor feels. The Great Physician, he who descended below all things during the awful hours of atonement (D&C 88:6; 122:8), is able, through his Holy Spirit, to reveal to his ordained servants what they need to know and feel in order to lead the wandering sheep back into the fold.

Lessons come to us from God through our challenges and distresses and setbacks and failures. Pain has a purifying work, a divine work that can transform the soul of the distressed one, *if* he or she approaches the difficulty with the proper attitude. It is not uncommon for those who have lost a loved one, or who face the prospects of a terminal disease, or whose financial fortunes have been dramatically reversed, to ask, "Why? Why would God do this to me? Why is this happening?" These are, of course, "natural" reactions to trauma, especially when we would be perfectly content to remain perfectly content. But that's not why we are here.

I have sometimes suggested to sufferers, as kindly and lovingly as I could, that "Why is this happening?" is not the proper question. Why *is* it happening? Because we are mortal, because things like this happen in a mortal world. No one of us is required by God to enjoy suffering or to anticipate with delight the next trial. An associate said to me once: "You know, Bob, I learn so much from my trials that I find myself praying that the Lord will send more trials my way." I smiled, but I thought, *No way! You wouldn't catch me praying for trials. They come without asking for them.* On the other hand, it makes little sense for us to come to earth to be proven and then to ask why we are being proven. The Father is the Husbandman, the Vinedresser. The Savior is the Vine, and we are the branches. The Vinedresser chooses the manner in which he will purge the branches. Why? "Every branch that beareth fruit," the Master stated, "he [the Father] purgeth it, that it may bring forth more fruit" (John 15:2).

Elder Richard G. Scott pointed out that "when you face adversity, you can be led to ask many questions. Some serve a useful purpose; others do not. To ask, Why does this have to happen to me? Why do I have to suffer this now? What have I done to cause this? will lead you into blind alleys. . . .

"Rather ask, What am I to do? What am I to learn from this experience? What am I to change? Whom am I to help? How can I remember my many blessings in times of trial?"[13]

Holocaust survivor Viktor Frankl wrote: "We who lived in concentration camps can remember the men who walked through the huts comforting others, giving away their last piece of bread. They may have been few in number, but they offer sufficient proof that everything can be taken from a man but one thing: the last of . . . human freedoms—to choose one's attitude in any given set of circumstances, [and] to choose one's own way [of life]."[14]

At a very difficult time for my wife, Shauna, and me—when we watched helplessly as loved ones chose painful and unproductive paths—we found ourselves, early in the process of dealing with the pain, at a crossroads. We sensed that our attitude toward what we were experiencing was everything. To be honest, both of us went through weeks and months in which our days were filled with self-doubt, with personal recrimination, with loads of questions about what we had done wrong over the years. But as we prayed with intensity, read scriptures with new and searching eyes, and spent time regularly in the holy temple, there began to distil upon us the quiet but powerful realization that only we could determine how we would deal with our situation. Would we allow our problems to strangle our marriage and family? Would we permit these difficulties to drive us into seclusion? Would we yield to doubt and cynicism, given that we had tried so hard through the years to do what we were asked?

I will be forever grateful that the two of us sensed that we had to face the challenge together and that the one thing we could not afford to have happen was for the trial to drive the two of us apart. Further, after a time of being wrung out emotionally and spiritually, we both recognized that the Lord was our only hope for peace, our only means of extricating ourselves from dysfunctional living. It was then that our prayers and our yearnings began to change. It was then that we found ourselves shorn of self-concern and naked in our ineptitude; it was then that we acknowledged our nothingness and drew upon the strength and lifting power of our Divine Redeemer. Of course we were still concerned, and we kept trying. But we were "trying in a new way, a less worried way."[15]

We should not be unnerved by trials and challenges and even a bad day once in a while. And there are certainly times when a third party, be it a priesthood leader, parent, trusted friend, or even a professional counselor, can assist us to put things in place or in proper perspective. It may even be necessary in some instances for an individual to have medication prescribed by a competent physician.

But we must never, ever, minimize the effect the Master can have in our lives, the calming and reassuring and healing balm that he can be to us, no matter the depth of our despair or the seriousness of our situation. "Whatever Jesus lays his hands upon lives," Elder Howard W. Hunter testified. "If Jesus lays his hands upon a marriage, it lives. If he is allowed to lay his hands on the family, it lives."[16] The touch of the Master's hand is life and light and love. It calms. It soothes. It sanctifies. It empowers. It transcends anything earthly. Those who have been healed by that sacred and sensitive touch are they who can joyously proclaim, as did Andrew, Simon Peter's brother, "We have found the Messias" (John 1:41).

I do not wish to minimize in any way the tremendous challenges that many of us face. They are real and sobering. I am very much aware that many today have been subjected to much pain and distress in their lives, to abuse, to neglect, to the agonies of wanting more than anything to live a normal life and to feel normal feelings but who seem unable to do so.

I know that the day is coming when all the wrongs, the awful wrongs of this life, will be righted, when the God of justice will attend to all evil. Things beyond our power to control will be corrected, either here or hereafter. Many of us may come to enjoy the lifting, liberating powers of the Atonement in this life, and all our losses will be made up before we pass from this sphere of existence. Perhaps some of us will wrestle all our days with traumas and trials, for he who orchestrates the events of our lives will surely fix the time of our release. I have a conviction that when a person passes through the veil of death, all impediments and challenges and crosses that were beyond his or her power to control—abuse, neglect, immoral environment, weighty traditions, etc.—will be removed, and perfect peace will prevail in our hearts.

While Shauna and I were going through our deepest sorrows and distresses, we could not have sensed what lessons for life were being chiseled into our souls. During that season of stress it all seemed so overwhelming, so awful, so terribly unfair. And as is true with most of us, it's tough to learn lessons while you're in the midst of the refiner's fire. Now, though I would not wish to go through that experience again, at the same time I would not trade the lessons we learned for anything in this world or the next. They were timeless lessons, eternal and tender tutorials that have drawn us closer to the Good Shepherd and expanded our consciousness and empathy for his precious sheep. We learned some things about God during those years of trial, and we also learned some things about ourselves. Fortunately or unfortunately, the only way I can know to what extent I will serve God at all hazards is for my mettle to be tested. Through being asked to offer his son Isaac, for example, Abraham needed to learn something about Abraham.

In some ways, then, facing our trials courageously and resolutely prepares us for fellowship with those who have passed the tests of mortality. Now, to be sure, The Church of Jesus Christ of Latter-day Saints does not teach that we should seek after either persecution or pain. But persecution and pain are the lot of the people of God in all ages, and each of us, saint and sinner alike, becomes acquainted with the Suffering Servant through our suffering. We have been taught, by One who knows best, that "all these things shall give thee experience, and shall be for thy good. The Son of Man hath descended below them all. Art thou greater than he?" (D&C 122:7–8).

No, we are not greater than he, nor should we suppose that fellowship with him who was well acquainted with grief will come to us through a life of ease. As the apostle Peter counseled us, "Beloved, think it not strange concerning the fiery trial which is to try you, as though some strange thing happened unto you: but rejoice, inasmuch as ye are partakers of Christ's sufferings; that, when his glory shall be revealed, ye may be glad also with exceeding joy" (1 Peter 4:12–13). Tough as it is, over time and through seasons of experience we come to glory in our trials, for only through times of weakness and distress do we eventually emerge into a day of strength and power (2 Corinthians 12:9–10). Further, we sense our need to address personally the problem of evil and suffering by attending to things over which we do have some control, namely, our own thoughts and actions. That is, "we must begin by acknowledging that evil isn't just *out there,* as some external threat against which we might heroically struggle, but also *in here,* in the recesses of our own hearts. Where do we begin to crusade against evil? In our own lives. As Marilyn McCord Adams challenges us, 'Continual repentance is . . . the best contribution [anyone] can make toward solving the problem of evil.'"[17]

THE VICTORY IS ASSURED

Several years ago Shauna and I struggled with how best to build faith in all of our children and how to entice wandering souls back into Church activity. A caring colleague, sensing the weight of my burdens, happened into my office one day and simply asked this question: "Do you think our Heavenly Father wanders through the heavens in morose agony over his straying children?"

Startled a bit, I thought for a moment and said, "No, I don't think so. I know he feels pain, but I honestly can't picture him living in eternal misery."

My friend responded, "Ask yourself why he does not do so, and it will bless your life."

I didn't get much work done the rest of the day, because I spent many hours pondering the question. When I arrived home that evening, I asked Shauna the same question. She answered as I did, and then the two of us set about a prayerful quest for the next several days to understand how our Eternal Father deals with his pain.

In time it dawned on us that the Lord knows the end from the beginning and that, as Joseph the Prophet declared, all things— past, present, and future—are and were with Him "one eternal now."[18] Perspective. PERSPECTIVE. That was the answer. God deals with pain through and by virtue of his infinite and perfect perspective. He not only knows what we have done and what we are doing but also what we will do in the future. If in fact, as the prophets have taught, many who are heirs to the blessings of the covenant made with Abraham, Isaac, and Jacob will in time or in eternity be reconciled to and reunited with the covenant family, then all we need to do for the time being is to seek through fasting and prayer for at least a portion of our God's perspective—his omniloving patience, his long-suffering, his ever-open arms, and a glimpse of the big picture. Such a perspective serves us well here, in the midst of our sufferings; it also empowers our souls and fashions us into the image of our Master, who is the personification and embodiment of charity, or the pure love of Christ (see Moroni 7:45–48).

Knowing something about the future can help us immeasurably in dealing responsibly and productively with the present. The reason we need not succumb to cynicism or depression or despair about how awful things are now is that one day, before very long, things will change. God is in charge. Satan may possess a huge following, and he may have great power, but God will win the battle between good and evil. As the apostle Paul declared, "Thanks be to God, [who] giveth us the victory through our Lord Jesus Christ" (1 Corinthians 15:57).

"Imagine that you are attending a football game," Elder Boyd K. Packer stated. "The teams seem evenly matched. One team has been trained to follow the rules; the other, to do just the opposite.

They are committed to cheat and disobey every rule of sportsman-like conduct.

"While the game ends in a tie, it is determined that it must continue until one side wins decisively.

"Soon the field is a quagmire.

"Players on both sides are being ground into the mud. The cheating of the opposing team turns to brutality.

"Players are carried off the field. Some have been injured critically; others, it is whispered, fatally. It ceases to be a game and becomes a battle.

"You become very frustrated and upset. 'Why let this go on? Neither team can win. It must be stopped.'

"Imagine that you confront the sponsor of the game and demand that he stop this useless, futile battle. You say it is senseless and without purpose. Has he no regard at all for the players?

"He calmly replies that he will not call the game. You are mistaken. There is a great purpose in it. You have not understood.

"He tells you that this is not a spectator sport—it is for the participants. It is for their sake that he permits the game to continue. Great benefit may come to them because of the challenges they face.

"He points to players sitting on the bench, suited up, eager to enter the game. 'When each one of them has been in, when each has met the day for which he has prepared so long and trained so hard, then, and only then, will I call the game.'

"Until then, it may not matter which team seems to be ahead. The present score is really not crucial. There are games within games, you know. Whatever is happening to the team, each player will have his day.

"Those players on the team that keeps the rules will not be eternally disadvantaged because they keep the rules. They may be cornered or misused, even defeated for a time. But individual players on that team, regardless of what appears on the scoreboard, may already be victorious.

"Each player will have a test sufficient to his needs; how each responds is the test.

"When the game is finally over, you and they will see purpose in it all, may even express gratitude for having been on the field during the darkest part of the contest."

Then, providing interpretation for this remarkable parable, Elder Packer added: "I do not think the Lord is quite so hopeless about what's going on in the world as we are. He could put a stop to all of it any moment. But He will not! Not until every player has a chance to meet the test for which we were preparing before the world was, before we came into mortality."[19]

It is true that perilous times lie ahead; that murder and immorality and deceit will extend their evil tentacles; that it will seem to us as though every man were at war with his neighbor. But there is safety in the stakes of Zion, safety within the gospel net, safety and security to be found through standing in holy places. While the prophetic promise is that the Lord will preserve his people (Moses 7:61), that does not necessarily mean the righteous will always be spared the pain of loss, the agony of misrepresentation and betrayal, or the sober reality of mortal death.[20]

Because we know that God will win, we need not fret about the future. Because we know that the great and abominable church will crumble, we need not be discouraged as organized evil spreads its mischief. Because we know that The Church of Jesus Christ of Latter-day Saints will indeed be found in every nation and kingdom under heaven, we need not worry about a slanderous remark or a misrepresentation of our faith and way of life. The Lord lives. This is his work, and he will bring it to consummation. He will not be defeated. Nephi prophesied: "For the time soon cometh that the fulness of the wrath of God shall be poured out upon all the children of men; for he will not suffer that the wicked shall destroy the righteous. Wherefore, he will preserve the righteous by his power, even if it so be that the fulness of his wrath must come, and the righteous be preserved, even unto the destruction of their enemies by fire," meaning, the fire of the glory of Christ at the time of his Second Coming. "Wherefore," Nephi continued, "the righteous need not fear; for thus saith the prophet, they shall be saved, even if it so be as by fire" (1 Nephi 22:16–17).

The Savior and his anointed servants have invited us to live and act today as the victors—with quiet confidence, with assurance, and with an optimism born not of arrogance but of trust in and reliance upon him who has all power. We can face the traumas of the present because we know something about what lies ahead. We proceed confidently in the war against evil because of our confidence in the Captain of our souls.

BEAUTY FOR ASHES

Some seven hundred years before the birth of Jesus of Nazareth, Isaiah uttered prophetic words that would find their fulfillment largely in the mortal ministry of the Anointed One: "The Spirit of the Lord God is upon me; because the Lord hath anointed me to preach good tidings unto the meek; he hath sent me *to bind up the brokenhearted, to proclaim liberty to the captives, and the opening of the prison to them that are bound;*

"To proclaim the acceptable year of the Lord, . . . *to comfort all that mourn;*

"To appoint unto them that mourn in Zion, *to give unto them beauty for ashes, the oil of joy for mourning,* the garment of praise for the spirit of heaviness" (Isaiah 61:1–3; emphasis added; compare Luke 4:18–19).

Jesus Christ came to earth to bring beauty for ashes—to replace distress with comfort, worry with peace, turmoil with rest. The

Good Shepherd came to earth on a search-and-rescue mission to identify and gather in those who have strayed, to welcome the wanderer back home and adorn the tattered son or daughter of God with a robe and a ring, to host a banquet with a fatted calf. Our precious Savior condescended—left his throne divine—to come down and be with his people, the sheep of his fold. He came to right all the terrible wrongs of this life, to fix the unfixable, to repair the irreparable. He came to heal us by his tender touch, to still the storms of our hearts. He came to replace ashes with beauty.

Because things do not always turn out as we expect, because today is not the day we bargained for, "every one of us," Elder Jeffrey R. Holland pointed out, "has times when we need to know things will get better. The Book of Mormon speaks of this as 'hope for a better world' [Ether 12:4]. For emotional health and spiritual stamina, everyone needs to be able to look forward to some respite, to do something pleasant and renewing and hopeful, whether that blessing be near at hand or still some distance ahead. . . .

"My declaration is that this is precisely what the gospel of Jesus Christ offers us, especially in times of need. There *is* help. There *is* happiness. There really *is* light at the end of the tunnel. It is the Light of the World. . . . I say: Hold on. Keep trying. God loves you. Things will improve. Christ comes to you in his 'more excellent ministry' with a future of 'better promises.'"[21]

Each one of us needs to know—needs the conviction, deep down in our souls—that our Master is not an absentee Landlord, not a distant Deity. He is "touched with the feeling of our infirmities" (Hebrews 4:15), knows from firsthand experience all about our pains, our afflictions, our temptations (Alma 7:11–12), and thereby understands "the weakness of man and how to succor them who are tempted" (D&C 62:1). He has not, as the deists proposed centuries ago, wound up the world clock and left it to run on its own. Rather, he is intimately involved in saving and succoring—literally, running to help—those who call upon him and learn to trust in his mighty arm. Indeed, our God's infinity does not preclude either his immediacy or his intimacy. As Enoch the seer learned, when we need God, when we reach out to him, he is there, his bosom is there; he is just and merciful and kind forever (Moses 7:30).

Many times we are tempted while in the crucible of suffering to cry out, Where is God? Where is he when we need him? Could he not have prevented this heinous deed? Our God, though an exalted Man of Holiness, is also all-powerful, has all knowledge, and is, by the power of his Spirit, everywhere present. He could, if he chose to do so, prevent every tragedy and block every trauma. But he will not do so, for such would thwart the great plan of happiness by impinging upon the moral agency of both the wicked and the righteous.

We are reminded that the Lord promises to give "the oil of joy for mourning, the garment of praise for the spirit of heaviness" (Isaiah 61:3). As we open ourselves to his redeeming and enabling power, Jesus pours oil on the troubled waters of our lives and clothes us in the quiet assurance of his sanctifying praise. When we have learned to lean on the Lord and rely on his goodness and his approval, then what the world thinks of us comes to matter precious little. When the fickle plaudits of the worldly wise no longer entice us, then we are buoyed up by the sweet peace that signals divine approval. "I receive not honour from men" (John 5:41), Jesus declared. And so it is with those who confess him as Lord and Master. We cry out: "Hear, O Lord, and have mercy upon me: Lord, be thou my helper. Thou hast turned for me my mourning into dancing: thou hast put off my sackcloth, and girded me with gladness" (Psalm 30:10–11).

We need not be free from turmoil or sorrow in order to be at rest in today's world. Like Nephi, we need not know the meaning of all things to know that the Savior loves us (1 Nephi 11:17) and that he can strengthen us to bear heavy burdens with relative ease.

The Lord is not slack in keeping his promises to his chosen people: he will give "beauty for ashes, the oil of joy for mourning, the garment of praise for the spirit of heaviness" (Isaiah 61:3). He will welcome his faithful Saints into "the rest of the Lord" (Moroni 7:3), both in granting them eternal life in the world to come and also in bestowing upon them in this life the peace that is the harbinger of eternal life (D&C 59:23), the peace in this life that passes all understanding (Philippians 4:7). God may not always remove us from the burdensome and toilsome circumstances in which we find ourselves, but he will empower us to deal responsibly with the circumstances and even to change them.

Conclusion

Life is good. I love life. Like you, I have experienced pain and fear and frustration and anguish of soul. Like you, I have had dark moments when I have asked, Why? Why am I being asked to pass through this miserable and unsettling situation, especially when I have tried so hard to do what's right? And so I know something about the sufferings and struggles that accompany life in this second estate. But many wonderful blessings are to be gained and lasting lessons to be learned through passing through the refiner's fire, particularly at this exciting time in earth's history. There is so much to look forward to. One day the God of justice will step into history and level the playing field.

"And one of the elders answered, saying unto me, What are these [people who] are arrayed in white robes? And whence came they?

"And I said unto him, Sir, thou knowest. And he said to me, These are they which came out of great tribulation, and have washed their robes, and made them white in the blood of the Lamb.

"Therefore are they before the throne of God, and serve him day and night in his temple: and he that sitteth on the throne shall dwell among them.

"They shall hunger no more, neither thirst any more; neither shall the sun light on them, nor any heat.

"For the Lamb which is in the midst of the throne shall feed them, and shall lead them unto living fountains of waters: and God shall wipe away all tears from their eyes" (Revelation 7:13–17).

I testify that the counsel of the prophets of God, ancient and modern, is true. We need not fear; we need not surrender to despair or doom and gloom. God is in his heavens. He knows us, one and all, and he knows of our pains and our possibilities. Jesus Christ our Deliverer lives, is directing his Church and kingdom through living prophets and apostles, and offers to bear our burdens and liberate our souls from the galling yoke of sin and the fetters of a fading world. I rejoice in the privilege it is to be a part of the dispensation of the fulness of times, to be a participant in the winding-up scenes. And I look forward, more than I can say, to the return in glory of our Lord and Savior and to life with him and the faithful Saints of all the ages of time.

CHAPTER TEN

THE BLESSINGS OF THE TEMPLE

Latter-day Saints take seriously the Savior's great commission, which is the obligation to take the message of salvation to all the world in order that every person might be invited to come unto Christ and be born of water and of the Spirit (John 3:5; Acts 2:37–38). And what of those who have died? What of those who never heard Jesus preach? What of those in the first century who did not hear the testimony of Peter or Nathaniel or Paul? And what of those who lived before or since that day, individuals throughout the earth who died ignorant of the gospel of Jesus Christ? Are they damned forever? Would God condemn his children to hell because they did not come unto a Christ they did not know or accept and receive covenants or ordinances of which they were unaware?

One distinctive belief of The Church of Jesus Christ of Latter-day Saints is baptism for the dead, a practice deriving from the concept that living mortal individuals may perform vicarious saving labors in behalf of those who have not had the opportunity to receive the same. This most unusual rite was begun by Joseph Smith during the Nauvoo period of our Church history at a time when there was no temple in which to perform the baptisms. Today, when we are witnessing a tremendous surge of growth in the number of temples throughout the earth, it seems appropriate to speak of this magnificent and transcendent vicarious service as one of the many marvelous fruits of the Restoration.

An Early Practice

Some time during or just after the mortal ministry of Jesus, the doctrine of salvation for the dead was revealed to the first-century Church. In chapter 15 of his first epistle to the Corinthians, the apostle Paul testifies of the resurrection of the Lord. Paul presents the core of that supernal message known to us as the gospel, or glad tidings, that Christ suffered for our sins, died, rose again the third day, and ascended into heaven. Joseph Smith called these events "the fundamental principles of our religion," to which all other doctrines are but appendages.[1] Paul showed the necessity for the Savior's rising from the tomb and explained that the physical evidence of the divine Sonship of Christ is the Resurrection. If Christ had not risen from the dead, Paul asserted, the preaching of the apostles and the faith of the Saints would be in vain. "If in this life only we have hope in Christ," he said, "we are of all men most miserable" (1 Corinthians 15:19).

After establishing that the Lord has conquered all enemies, including death, Paul declared: "And when all things shall be subdued unto him, then shall the Son also himself be subject unto him [the Father] that put all things under him, that God may be all in all. Else what shall they do which are baptized for the dead, *if the dead rise not at all? why are they then baptized for the dead?*" (1 Corinthians 15:28–29; emphasis added).

Verse 29 has given rise to a host of interpretations by biblical scholars of various faiths. Many consider the original meaning of the passage to be at best "difficult" or "unclear." One commentator stated that Paul here "alludes to a practice of the Corinthian community as evidence for Christian faith in the resurrection of the dead. . . . It seems that in Corinth some Christians would undergo baptism in the name of their deceased non-Christian relatives and friends, hoping that this vicarious baptism might assure them a share in the redemption of Christ."[2]

Some recent translations of the Bible have attempted to clarify this passage. The New King James Version renders it: "Otherwise, what will they do who are baptized for the dead, if the dead do not rise at all? Why then are they baptized for the dead?" The Revised English Bible translates 1 Corinthians 15:29: "Again, there are those who receive baptism on behalf of the dead. What do you suppose they are doing? If the dead are not raised to life at all, what do they mean by being baptized on their behalf?"

One commentator noted that "it is difficult to imagine any circumstances under which Paul would think it permissible for living Christians to be baptized for the sake of unbelievers in general. Such a view, adopted in part by the Mormons, lies totally outside the NT understanding both of salvation and of baptism."[3] Many scholars of other faiths believe that in 1 Corinthians Paul was denouncing or condemning the practice of baptism for the dead as heretical.[4] Latter-day Saints consider that a strange conclusion, because Paul uses the practice to support the doctrine of the resurrection. In essence, he says, "Why are we performing baptism in behalf of our dead, if, as some propose, there will be no resurrection of the dead? If there is to be no resurrection, would not such baptisms be a waste of time?"

On the subject of baptism for the dead, one scholar of another faith observed: "Paul had no reason to mention baptism for the dead unless he thought it would be an effective argument with the Corinthians, so presumably he introduced what he thought was an inconsistency in the Corinthians' theology. In this case, some at

Corinth might have rejected an afterlife but practiced baptism for the dead, not realizing what the rite implied." In addition, "because his mention [of the practice] could imply his toleration or approval of it, many have tried to distance Paul from baptism for the dead or remove features regarded as offensive from it. Some maintain that Paul was arguing *ad hominem* or *ex concessu* in 1 Cor 15:29, so that he neither approved nor disapproved of the practice by referring to it. Yet it would have been unlike Paul to refrain from criticizing a practice he did not at least tolerate."[5] Or as an LDS New Testament scholar pointed out: "Paul was most sensitive to blasphemy and false ceremonialism—of all people he would not have argued for the foundation truth of the Resurrection with a questionable example. He obviously did not feel that the principle was disharmonious with the gospel."[6]

The doctrine of salvation for the dead was known and understood by ancient Christian communities. Early commentators on the statement in Hebrews that "they without us should not be made perfect" (Hebrews 1 1:40) hold that the passage referred to the Old Testament Saints who were trapped in Hades awaiting the help of their New Testament counterparts and that Christ held the keys that would "open the doors of the Underworld to the faithful souls there."[7] Justin Martyr, in his work called Dialogue with Trypho, cites a passage that he charges had been deleted from the book of Jeremiah but was still to be found in some synagogue copies of the text: "The Lord God remembered His dead ones, who slept in the earth of dust, Israel who lay in the graves; and He descended to preach to them His salvation."[8] Irenaeus also taught: "The Lord descended to the parts under the earth, announcing to them also the good news of His coming; there being remission of sins for such as believe on Him."[9]

An early Christian document linking the writings of Peter on Christ's ministry in the spirit world (see 1 Peter 3:18–20; 4:6) to those of Paul on baptism for the dead is the Shepherd of Hermas, which states that "these apostles and teachers who preached the name of the Son of God, having fallen asleep in the power and faith of the Son of God, preached also to those who had fallen asleep before them, and themselves gave to them the seal of the preaching. *They went down therefore with them into the water and came up again,* but the latter went down alive and came up alive, while the former, who had fallen asleep before, went down dead but came up alive. *Through them, therefore, they were made alive, and received the knowledge of the name of the Son of God.*"[10]

Similarly, another apocryphal New Testament document, the Gospel of Peter, speaks of the singular moment in Christian history when the tomb was opened at the time of the resurrection of our Lord. "When the soldiers saw these things, they woke up the centurion and the elders—for they were also there on guard. As they were explaining what they had seen, they saw three men emerge from the tomb, two of them supporting the other, with a cross following behind them. The heads of the two reached up to the sky, but the head of the one they were leading went up above the skies." Then we come to the following strange but fascinating account: "And they heard a voice from the skies, 'Have you preached to those who are asleep?' And a reply came from the cross, 'Yes.'"[11]

In a modern commentary on 1 Peter, author Leonhard Goppelt observes that 1 Peter 3:19 and 4:6 are the only passages in the New Testament that refer to the ministry of Christ to the postmortal spirit world. He points out that "1 Peter would not be able to make such brief reference to this idea if it were not already known in the churches as tradition. What 1 Peter says in regard to this tradition is, in comparison with the traditions of the second century, quite 'apostolic.'" Through this means, "the saving effectiveness of [the Lord's] suffering unto death extends even to those mortals who in earthly life do not come to a conscious encounter with him, even to the most lost among them."[12]

AN ANCIENT PRACTICE RESTORED

Joseph Smith observed: "Aside from knowledge independent of the Bible, I would say that it [baptism for the dead] was certainly practiced by the ancient churches. . . .

"The Saints have the privilege of being baptized for those of their relatives who are dead, whom they believe would have embraced the Gospel, if they had been privileged with hearing it, and who have received the Gospel in the spirit [world], through the instrumentality of those who have been commissioned to preach to them."[13] On another occasion he taught, "If we can, by the authority of the Priesthood of the Son of God, baptize a man in the name of the Father, of the Son, and of the Holy Ghost, for the remission of sins, it is just as much our privilege to act as an agent, and be baptized for the remission of sins for and in behalf of our dead kindred, who have not heard the Gospel, or the fulness of it."[14]

This is what Peter meant when he wrote: "For Christ also hath once suffered for sins, the just for the unjust, that he might bring us to God, being put to death in the flesh, but quickened by the Spirit: by which also *he went and preached unto the spirits* in prison." Further, "*For this cause was the gospel preached also to them that are dead,* that they might be judged according to men in the flesh, but live according to God in the spirit" (1 Peter 3:18–19; 4:6; emphasis added). In short, we believe that every person will have the opportunity, either in this life or the next, to receive the fulness of the gospel of Jesus Christ and enter into the everlasting covenant.

Canon Frederic W. Farrar, writing in the nineteenth century, observed that "St. Peter has one doctrine that is almost peculiar to himself, and which is inestimably precious." This doctrine, Farrar explained, is a "much disregarded and, indeed, till recent times, half-forgotten article of the Christian creed; I mean the object of Christ's descent into Hades. In this truth is involved nothing less than the extension of Christ's redeeming work to the dead who died before his coming. Had the Epistle contained nothing else but this, it would at once have been raised above the irreverent charge of being 'secondhand and commonplace.'" Farrar then quoted two passages from 1 Peter (3:18–20; 4:6) and said, "Few words of Scripture have been so tortured and emptied of their significance as these." He noted that "every effort has been made to explain away the plain meaning of this passage. It is one of the most precious passages of Scripture, and it involves no ambiguity, except such as is created by the scholasticism of a prejudiced theology. It stands almost alone in Scripture. . . . For if language have any meaning, this language means that Christ, when His spirit descended into the lower world, proclaimed the message of salvation to the once impenitent dead." In broadening our perspective beyond those of the days of Noah, Farrar wrote, "It is impossible to suppose that the antediluvian sinners, conspicuous as they were for their wickedness, were the only ones of all the dead who were singled out to receive the message of deliverance." Continuing, this respected churchman pointed out: "We thus rescue the work of redemption from the appearance of having failed to achieve its end for the vast majority of those for whom Christ died. By accepting the light thus thrown upon 'the descent into Hell,' we extend to those of the dead who have not finally hardened themselves against it the blessedness of Christ's atoning work." Further, Farrar wrote that "we do not press the inference of Hermas and St. Clemens of Alexandria by teaching that this passage implies also other missions of Apostles and Saints to the world of spirits."[15]

Between the time of Christ's death on the cross and his rising from the tomb, he went into the postmortal spirit world, preached his gospel, and organized the faithful so that the message of truth might be made available to all who are willing to receive it (see D&C 138). But because the sacraments or ordinances of the Church are earthly ordinances and therefore must be performed on this side of the veil of death, Latter-day Saints go into temples to receive the sacraments in behalf of those who have died without them. "Every man," Joseph Smith pointed out, "that has been baptized and belongs to the kingdom has a right to be baptized for those who have gone before; and as soon as the law of the Gospel is obeyed here by their friends who act as proxy for them, the Lord has administrators there [in the spirit world] to set them free."[16] He also taught: "Jesus Christ became a ministering spirit (while His body was lying in the sepulcher) to the spirits in prison, to fulfill an important part of His mission, without which He could not have perfected His work, or entered into his rest. . . . It is no more incredible that God should *save* the dead, than that he should *raise* the dead."[17] Thus Latter-day Saints feel the need to be anxiously engaged in the work of the ministry on both sides of the veil.

More often than not, baptism for the dead, together with other temple ordinances, is considered by traditional Christians to be an unnecessary, ill-advised, or even contemptible practice. In the 10 August 1998 issue of *Christianity Today,* a reader inquired: "I've heard Mormons criticized for getting 'baptized for the dead,' but in 1 Corinthians 15:29, Paul writes [quotes the verse]. Did Jews or early Christians practice this? Why do we believe it's wrong to practice it today?"

D. A. Carson, a respected biblical scholar, responded briefly with familiar arguments against the practice: the doctrine is mentioned in only one place in the Bible; Paul uses the word *they* (rather than *we*) in referring to the practice, thus implying that he was not associated with the practice; and, in short, "there is no good evidence for vicarious baptism anywhere in the New Testament or among the earliest apostolic fathers. . . . If the practice existed at all, it may have been tied to a few people or special cases—for example, when a relative died after trusting the gospel but before being baptized. We really do not know."[18] In a Christian world where people are not persuaded that baptism in *the flesh* is necessary for entrance into the Lord's Church and thus essential to salvation or where baptism is viewed as some extraneous and nonessential work that somehow undercuts or compromises the saving grace of the Lord, we should not be surprised about some of the reactions to this doctrine and practice.

In Zion the center of all religious activity is the temple. Like Israel of old, the ritual and religion of the holy temple give broadened meaning to all that is undertaken in Zion. Indeed, the crowning tie to Israel comes only by the worthy reception of the blessings of the temple, through the endowment and the sealing of family units (see D&C 131:1–4). "What was the [ultimate] object," Joseph Smith asked, "of gathering the Jews, or the people of God, in any age of the world?" He then answered: "*The main object was to build unto the Lord a house whereby He could reveal unto His people the ordinances of His house and the glories of His kingdom,* and teach the people the way of salvation; for there are certain ordinances and principles that, when they are taught and practiced, must be done in a place or house built for that purpose."[19] "Missionary work," Elder Russell M. Nelson observed, "is only the beginning" to the blessings of Abraham, Isaac, and Jacob. "The fulfillment, the consummation, of these blessings comes as those who have entered the waters of baptism perfect their lives to the point that they may enter the holy temple. Receiving an endowment there seals members of the Church to the Abrahamic Covenant."[20]

ENDOWED FROM ON HIGH

The unfolding of divine truth and priesthood authority, including temple rites and ordinances, came line upon line, precept upon precept. John the Baptist, the prophet about whom the Savior stated that there was none greater (Luke 7:28), appeared to Joseph Smith and Oliver Cowdery on 15 May 1829. John, who linked two major dispensations—ending the Mosaic and initiating the Messianic—ordained Joseph and Oliver priests and conferred upon them the keys of the Aaronic Priesthood, thus strengthening our link to the past (D&C 13).[21] Peter, James, and John, who were taught and ordained by the Lord Jesus and who also received keys at the hands of the ancient prophets Moses and Elias on the Mount of Transfiguration (Matthew 17:1–9),[22] appeared a few weeks later to restore apostolic authority and the keys of the Priesthood of Melchizedek (D&C 18:9; 20:3; 27:12; 128:20). The Church was organized on 6 April 1830 with Joseph and Oliver as its first and second elders. The first high priests were ordained in June 1831, the First Presidency was established in 1833, and the Quorum of the Twelve Apostles and the First Quorum of the Seventy were put in place in February 1835.

The Saints were instructed very early that "ye are to be taught from on high. Sanctify yourselves and ye shall be endowed with power, that ye may give even as I have spoken" (D&C 43:16). Further, in the revelation we know as the Olive Leaf (D&C 88), the Lord provided instructions for the School of the Prophets, instructions that anticipated temple worship: "Sanctify yourselves; yea, purify your hearts, and cleanse your hands and your feet before me, that I may make you clean." In addition, the early leaders were told to "organize yourselves; prepare every needful thing; and establish a house, even a house of prayer, a house of fasting, a house of faith, a house of learning, a house of glory, a house of order, a house of God" (D&C 88:74, 119; compare 109:14–16).

On 12 November 1835 the Prophet Joseph met with the Twelve. Among other things, he said: "The house of the Lord must be prepared, and the solemn assembly called and organized in it, according to the order of the house of God. . . .

" . . . The order of the house of God has been, and ever will be, the same, even after Christ comes; and after the termination of the thousand years it will be the same; and we shall finally enter into the celestial kingdom of God, and enjoy it forever." He added: "You need an endowment, brethren, in order that you may be prepared and able to overcome all things."[23]

The endowment promised to the Latter-day Saints was like the endowment promised to the Former-day Saints. Just before his ascent into heaven, Jesus said to his meridian Twelve: "I send the promise of my Father upon you: but tarry ye in the city of Jerusalem, until ye be endued [clothed, invested] with power from on high" (Luke 24:49; see also Acts 1:4). In our day that same Lord declared: "I gave unto you a commandment that you should build a house, in the which house I design to endow those whom I have chosen with power from on high; for this is the promise of the Father unto you; therefore I command you to tarry, even as mine apostles at Jerusalem" (D&C 95:8–9). The endowment in the first-century Christian Church, like the endowment in the Restored Church, was two-fold: an unusual outpouring of the Spirit of God and participation in sacred temple ordinances.

We are told by Luke that Jesus "shewed himself alive after his passion [suffering] by many infallible proofs, being seen of them forty days, and speaking of the things pertaining to the kingdom of God" (Acts 1:3). Robert J. Matthews has suggested that it may have been during the Savior's forty-day ministry, following his resurrection but before his final ascension, that the full-fledged church organization (later spoken of by Paul in Ephesians 4:11–14) came into being.[24] It is fascinating to discover such ordinances as washings, anointings, sacred clothing, new names, and sacred marriage ceremonies mentioned in what is known as the apocryphal Forty-day Literature.[25] The day of Pentecost stands as the scriptural reminder of the baptism by fire that came to the early Christians. On that occasion they preached, prophesied, and spoke in tongues, inspired and divinely empowered in a way that they had not hitherto known or experienced (Acts 2). This outpouring, combined with their encounter with the resurrected Lord, transformed a group of simple and fearful disciples into powerful, indefatigable witnesses of the work. According to Willard Richards, Joseph the Prophet taught that "at one time God obtained a house where Peter washed and anointed, etc., on the day of Pentecost."[26]

A similar outpouring of the Spirit took place among the Latter-day Saints. Professor Milton V. Backman Jr. has written: "During a fifteen-week period, extending from January 21 to May 1, 1836, probably more Latter-day Saints beheld visions and witnessed other unusual spiritual manifestations than during any other era in the history of the Church. There were reports of Saints' beholding heavenly beings at ten different meetings held during that time. At eight of these meetings, many reported seeing angels; and at five of the services, individuals testified that Jesus, the Savior, appeared. While the Saints were thus communing with heavenly hosts, many prophesied, some spoke in tongues, and others received the gift of interpretation of tongues."[27]

The second part of the Lord's promise, the ordinance of the endowment, as now administered in Latter-day Saint temples, came to us, as did all of the truths of the Restoration, line upon line. The Saints in Kirtland participated in what we have come to know as a partial endowment, consisting of washings, anointings, sealing of anointings, and washing of feet.[28] Further, Joseph Smith's vision of the celestial kingdom (D&C 137), received on 21 January 1836, unlocked one of the mysteries of eternity—the blessed concept that the work of the salvation of souls continues after this life is over; the work of the Lord goes forward, here and hereafter. This vision opened the door to the doctrine of the redemption of the dead. Four years later the Prophet would speak of baptism for the dead in a public sermon, at the funeral of Seymour Brunson on 15 August 1840,[29] but the foundation was laid. Further, Moses, Elias, and Elijah came in April 1836 (D&C 110) to restore invaluable keys associated with the organization and formation and sealing of eternal family units. Moses restored the keys of the gathering of Israel. Elias restored the keys associated with establishing eternal family units through the blessings of celestial marriage, the new and everlasting covenant of marriage, which was the marriage covenant of Abraham, Isaac, and Jacob. And Elijah restored the fulness of the priesthood, power and keys sufficient to seal individuals and families together forever.[30]

ENDOWED IN NAUVOO

The Prophet's confinement in Liberty Jail in the winter of 1838–39, though hellish in hunger, privation, and alienation, proved a great blessing to the Saints through its spiritual impact on Joseph Smith. The months of solitude in what Elder B. H. Roberts called the "prison-temple"[31] were also months of sacred surrender and deep, prayerful reflection upon things of eternal worth, a type of spiritual gestation. The relatively peaceful years in Nauvoo resulted in tremendous outpourings of light and truth, in great doctrinal development, in formal revelations as well as public discourses. Elder Neal A. Maxwell pointed out that "earlier, Joseph had Oliver Cowdery and Sidney Rigdon to be not only his *aides-de-camp* but also in a measure as his spokesmen. After the Liberty Jail experience, however, Joseph was clearly his own spokesman. From that time forward, we begin to receive Joseph's stretching sermons, involving some of the gospel's most powerful doctrines."[32] And of course among the most profound of his revelations was the expanded temple endowment in Nauvoo.

In a revelation received on 19 January 1841, the Lord gave the Saints instructions to build a temple in Nauvoo. The Saints were to "build a house to my name, for the Most High to dwell therein. For there is not a place found on earth that he may come to and again restore that which was lost unto you, or which he hath taken away, even the fulness of the priesthood" (D&C 124:27–28). The Lord went on to say that the ordinance of baptism for the dead belongs "to my house, and cannot be acceptable to me, only in the days of your poverty, wherein ye are not able to build a house unto me. But I command you, all ye my saints, to build a house unto me; and I grant unto you a sufficient time to build a house unto me; and during this time your baptisms [performed in the Mississippi River or in a portable font] shall be acceptable unto me" (D&C 124:30–31). Through the blessings of the temple the people of the covenant would come to know "things which have been kept hid from before the foundation of the world, things that pertain to the dispensation of the fulness of times" (D&C 124:41).

Lucius Scovill recalled the following: "I can testify that on the third of May, 1842, Joseph Smith the Prophet called upon five or six, viz: Shadrach Roundy, Noah Rogers, Dimick B. Huntington, Daniel Cairns, and myself (I am not certain but that Hosea Stout was there also) to meet with him (the Prophet) in his business office (the upper part of his brick store). He told us that his object he had for us was to go to work and fit up that room preparatory to giving endowments to a few Elders that he might give unto them all the keys of power pertaining to the Aaronic and Melchizedek Priesthoods.

"We therefore went to work making the necessary preparations, and everything was arranged representing the interior of a temple as much as the circumstances would permit, he being with us dictating everything. He gave us many items that were very interesting to us, which sank with deep weight upon my mind, especially after the temple was finished at Nauvoo, and I had received the ordinances in which I was among the first, as I had been called upon to work in the temple as one of the hands during the winter. Some weeks previous to the dedication he told us we should have the privilege of receiving the whole of the ordinances in due time. The history of Joseph Smith speaks for itself. But I can and do testify that I know of a surety that room was fitted up by his order which we finished in the forenoon of the said 4th of May 1842. And he gave us to understand that he intended to have everything done by him that was in his power while he remained with us. He said his work was nearly done and he should roll the burden of the kingdom upon the shoulders of the Twelve. I am the only one living that I know of, who helped to fit up that room, except Hosea Stout, [who] was there."[33]

The following is from the journal of the Prophet Joseph Smith under date of 4 May 1842:

"I spent the day in the upper part of the store, that is in my private office . . . in council with General James Adams, of Springfield, Patriarch Hyrum Smith, Bishops Newel K. Whitney and George Miller, and President Brigham Young and Elders Heber C. Kimball and Willard Richards, instructing them in the principles and order of the Priesthood, attending to washings, anointings, endowments and the communication of keys pertaining to the Aaronic Priesthood, and so on to the highest order of the Melchizedek Priesthood, setting forth the order pertaining to the Ancient of Days, and all those plans and principles by which any one is enabled to secure the fulness of those blessings which have been prepared for the Church of the Firstborn, and come up and abide in the presence of the Eloheim in the eternal worlds. In this council was instituted the ancient order of things for the first time in these last days. And the communications I made to this council were of things spiritual, and to be received only by the spiritual minded: and there was nothing made known to these men but what will be made known to all the Saints of the last days, so soon as they are prepared to receive, and a proper place is prepared to communicate them, even to the weakest of the Saints; therefore let the Saints be diligent in building the Temple, and all houses which they have been, or shall hereafter be, commanded of God to build; and wait their time with patience in all meekness, faith, perseverance unto the end, knowing assuredly that all these things referred to in this council are always governed by the principle of revelation."[34]

In the months that followed, Joseph Smith spoke repeatedly in public discourses of sealing powers and ordinances; indeed, he was focused on preparing his people for what lay ahead by initiating them into the mysteries of godliness associated with the everlasting perpetuation of the family. It is not surprising to learn, therefore, that the Prophet's most quoted biblical passage was Malachi 4:5–6. In the fall of 1843 he began to deliver the fulness of the blessings of the priesthood. He explained that "if a man gets a fulness of the priesthood of God he has to get it in the same way that Jesus Christ obtained it, and that was by keeping all the commandments and obeying all the ordinances of the house of the Lord."[35] Further, "those holding the fulness of the Melchizedek Priesthood are kings and priests of the Most High God, holding the keys of power and blessings."[36] He held out the supernal hope to parents that "when a seal is put upon the father and mother, it secures their posterity, so that they cannot be lost, but will be saved by virtue of the covenant of their father and mother."[37]

As we know, Joseph the Seer did not live to see the Nauvoo Temple completed and dedicated. The duty of administering the endowment to thousands of Saints before the exodus devolved upon President Brigham Young and the Quorum of the Twelve Apostles. But before his martyrdom, the Prophet and the Twelve met in long, extended sessions in which divine truths and saving powers were delivered. On one occasion, Elder Wilford Woodruff recorded that the Prophet said to the apostles: "'I have sealed upon your heads all the keys of the kingdom of God. I have sealed upon you every key, power, [and] principle that the God of heaven has revealed to me. Now, no matter where I may go or what I may do, the kingdom rests upon you.' . . . 'But,' . . . 'ye apostles of the Lamb of God, my brethren, upon your shoulders this kingdom rests; now you have got to round up your shoulders and bear off the kingdom.' . . . 'If you do not do it you will be damned.'"[38] Thus, in reality, there was no "succession crisis" at the time of the Martyrdom, except in the minds of those who did not (or who do not today) understand the nature of apostolic succession and the keys of the kingdom of God.

CONCLUSION

The good news, or glad tidings, of salvation in Christ is intended to lift our sights and bring hope to our souls, to "bind up the brokenhearted, to proclaim liberty to the captives, and the opening of the prison to them that are bound" (Isaiah 61:1). That hope in Christ is in the infinite capacity of an infinite Being to save all mankind from ignorance as well as from sin and death. The God of Abraham, Isaac, and Jacob is indeed the God of the living (Matthew 22:32), and his influence and redemptive mercies span the veil of death (1 Corinthians 15:19).

And so what of those who have not had the opportunity in this life to know of Christ and his gospel, who have not had the opportunity to be baptized for a remission of sins and for entrance into the kingdom of God, who have not had the privilege of being bound in marriage and sealed in the family unit? In a world gripped by cynicism and strangled by hopelessness, the Latter-day Saints teach of a God of mercy and vision, of an Omnipotent One whose reach to his children is neither deterred by distance nor dimmed by death.

"There is never a time," Joseph Smith stated, "when the spirit is too old to approach God. All are within reach of pardoning mercy, who have not committed the unpardonable sin. . . .

"This glorious truth [baptism for the dead] is well calculated to enlarge the understanding, and to sustain the soul under troubles, difficulties and distresses. For illustration, suppose the case of two men, brothers, equally intelligent, learned, virtuous and lovely, walking in uprightness and in all good conscience, so far as they have been able to discern duty from the muddy stream of tradition, or from the blotted page of the book of nature.

"One dies and is buried, having never heard the Gospel of rec-onciliation; to the other the message of salvation is sent, he hears and embraces it, and is made the heir of eternal life. Shall the one become the partaker of glory and the other be consigned to hope-less perdition? Is there no chance for his escape? Sectarianism answers 'none.' Such an idea is worse than atheism."[39]

"It was at this time [in Philadelphia in 1839] that I received from [Joseph Smith] the first idea of eternal family organization," Elder Parley P. Pratt recalled, "and the eternal union of the sexes in those inexpressibly endearing relationships which none but the highly intellectual, the refined and pure in heart, know how to prize, and which are at the very foundation of everything worthy to be called happiness.

"Till then I had learned to esteem kindred affections and sym-pathies as appertaining solely to this transitory state, as something from which the heart must be entirely weaned, in order to be fit-ted for its heavenly state.

"It was Joseph Smith who taught me how to prize the endearing relationships of father and mother, husband and wife; of brother and sister, son and daughter.

"It was from him that I learned that the wife of my bosom might be secured to me for time and all eternity; and that the refined sympathies and affections which endeared us to each other emanated from the fountain of divine eternal love. It was from him that I learned that we might cultivate these affections, and grow and increase in the same to all eternity. . . .

"I had loved before, but I knew not why. But now I loved—with a pureness—an intensity of elevated, exalted feeling, which would lift my soul from the transitory things of this grovelling sphere and expand it as the ocean. I felt that God was my heavenly Father indeed; that Jesus was my brother, and that the wife of my bosom was an immortal, eternal companion; a kind ministering angel, given to me as a comfort, and a crown of glory for ever and ever. In short, I could now love with the spirit and with the understanding also."[40]

My heart aches as I read the words or listen to the sermons of good men and women, devoted and intelligent religious leaders, who do not grasp the beauty of the concept of the eternal family, who do not fathom what things are possible through the powers of the holy priesthood. My heart leaps and my joy is full as I reflect upon what takes place in holy temples in regard to both the living and the dead. President Howard W. Hunter pleaded with us: "I invite the Latter-day Saints to look to the temple of the Lord as the great symbol of your membership. It is the deepest desire of my heart to have every member of the Church worthy to enter the temple. . . . The things that we must do and not do to be worthy of a temple recommend are the very things that ensure we will be happy as individuals and as families."[41]

President Gordon B. Hinckley has taught: "These unique and wonderful buildings, and the ordinances administered therein, represent the ultimate in our worship. These ordinances become the most profound expressions of our theology. . . . I am satisfied that every man or woman who goes to the temple in a spirit of sincerity and faith leaves the house of the Lord a better man or woman."[42]

"The crowning blessings of the gospel," Elder Bruce R. McConkie observed, "are received in temples, in holy sanctuaries apart from the world, in the places where only the faithful assemble. It is in temples . . . that the saints receive the mysteries of godliness. It is in these holy houses that faithful couples enter into the ordinance of celestial marriage through which they become parties to the Abrahamic covenant, the covenant of eternal increase, the covenant that in them and in their seed all generations shall be blessed."[43]

The temple is a place of eternal linking. It links—

- the heavens and the earth;
- the past, the present, and the future;
- time and eternity;
- husbands and wives, parents and children;
- the living and the dead; and,
- men and women to Jesus Christ and to the Father.

Temples point us back to the beginning; they affirm our lineal and doctrinal connection to the ancients. Truly, the course of the Lord is one eternal round (1 Nephi 10:19), for "this same Priesthood, which was in the beginning, shall be in the end of the world also" (Moses 6:7).

Temples point to things in this life that are of saving worth; they provide a firm but gentle and loving reminder of what matters most. Temples direct us to the world to come; they focus our minds on the truth that life and love and learning are forever, that glory and honor and immortality and eternal lives await the faithful.

CHAPTER ELEVEN

THE LIVING CANON

Jews, Christians, and Muslims all possess sacred writings and are loyal to those writings, their canon of scripture. The Jews have what we call the Old Testament and what they know as the Hebrew Bible, or Torah. Traditional Christians have the Old Testament and the New Testament. The Muslims have the Bible and the Koran. Latter-day Saint Christians have the Bible, the Book of Mormon, the Doctrine and Covenants, and the Pearl of Great Price. The root meaning of the word *canon* is "reed" and seems to have been understood to refer to a type of ruler or measuring device or (later, in a metaphorical sense) a standard—thus our phrase "standard works." Origen, the great Alexandrian scholar (A.D. 184–254), used *canon* to refer to what "we call the 'rule of faith,' the standard by which we are to measure and evaluate everything that may be offered to us as an article of belief. In this sense the word is closely linked with the authority of Scripture."[1] In another sense, *canon* came to be associated with a list or index or collection of documents that served as the rule of faith, though such a use of the word seems not to have been made earlier than Athanasius (A.D. 296–373).

F. F. Bruce, that great Christian scholar, was quick to distinguish between the canonicity of a book and its authority: "Its canonicity is dependent upon its authority. For when we ascribe canonicity to a book we simply mean that it belongs to the canon or list. But why does it so belong? Because it was recognized as possessing special authority. People frequently speak and write as if the authority with which the books of the Bible are invested in the minds of Christians is the result of their having been included in the sacred list. But the historical fact is the other way about; they were and are included in the list because they were acknowledged as authoritative." He concludes by stating simply, "Both logically and historically, authority precedes canonicity."[2]

Applying the Rule of Faith

Some scholars have suggested five guiding principles to determine whether a book belongs within the canon of scripture:

"(1) Is it *authoritative*—did it come with the authority of God? (2) Is it *prophetic*—was it written by a man of God? (3) Is it *authentic*—did it tell the truth about God, man, etc.? (4) Is it *dynamic*—did it come with the life-transforming power of God? (5) Was it *received,* collected, read and used—was it accepted by the people of God?"[3]

Several factors point out the need for a canon of Old Testament scripture. For one thing, the Jewish sacrificial system was ended with the destruction of Jerusalem and the temple in A.D. 70. The Jews were scattered, and they needed to determine which books were the authoritative word of God because of the extrascriptural writings of the time. Exiled Jews returned to ancient scripture to rekindle their hope of deliverance and reestablishment as a nation, all of which had been the burden of so many Old Testament prophets. Thus, "for the study and preservation of this the synagogue arose, and Judaism was enabled to survive the destruction of its Temple and the interruption of its national worship."[4]

The debates raged for centuries on what constituted scripture. There was, for example, repeated dispute on the status of such books as Proverbs, Ecclesiastes, the Song of Solomon, and Esther. The book of Esther did not contain the name of God; Ecclesiastes was difficult to square with contemporary orthodoxy. The Synod at Jamnia, which took place about A.D. 90, proved to be critical in the review and collection of these works and others that came to be the twenty-two books of the Hebrew Bible.[5]

It is interesting to note Christ's reference to the canon of scripture in the meridian of time. In the Upper Room, after the Resurrection, he spoke to the disciples regarding the scriptures as a witness to his divine Sonship: "These are the words which I spake unto you, while I was yet with you, that all things must be fulfilled, which were written in the law of Moses, and in the prophets, and in the psalms, concerning me" (Luke 24:44). Jesus was referring to the threefold division of the Hebrew Bible—the Law, the Prophets, and the Writings (although he called the Writings "the psalms" here, probably because the book of Psalms is the first and longest book in the third section). It appears that by the time of Jamnia a sort of unofficial canonization had been accomplished, so that "the Council of Jamnia," as one writer has indicated, "was the confirming of public opinion, not the forming of it."[6]

Though there seems to be no evidence of a dispute between Jesus and the Jews with regard to the canonicity of any Old Testament book, one clarification by the Prophet Joseph Smith in his inspired translation attests that at least some of the "plain and precious truths" of scripture had been taken away or kept back by the Savior's day: "Woe unto you, lawyers! For ye have taken away the key of knowledge, the *fulness of the scriptures;* ye enter not in yourselves into the kingdom; and those who were entering in, ye hindered" (JST Luke 11:53; emphasis added).

Another matter resolved (or confirmed) at Jamnia was the status of the Apocrypha, fourteen books that the Jews excluded from the Old Testament. Jerome, a fourth-century Church Father, was the first to call certain works *apocryphal,* meaning "secret or hidden." When Martin Luther finished his translation of the Bible in 1534, he placed the Old Testament apocryphal books in a group by themselves at the end of the Old Testament. This same pattern was followed by Myles Coverdale in 1535 in the first Bible printed in English. "Thereafter all the great historic English Bibles followed the same procedure. . . . Only in the Catholic Old Testament of 1610, which was translated from the Latin Vulgate," did the apocryphal books remain scattered throughout the Old Testament, as they are today in the Douai Version of the Bible.[7]

There were at least three reasons for determining a New Testament canon. First was the problem of heresy. For example, Marcion, a teacher from Asia Minor, went to Rome (A.D. 140) with a novel approach to the teaching of the gospel. Marcion rejected the Old Testament and proposed to substitute in its place a new canon consisting of two parts: the Gospel and the Apostle. The Gospel would be represented by an expurgated Gospel of Luke, and the Apostle would contain the Pauline letters, excluding Timothy and Titus. "Even the books which he did accept as canonical Scripture were edited in accordance with what he believed to be pure Christian doctrine. No doubt he believed that by this process of editing he was removing interpolations introduced by those who followed the teaching of the Twelve, as distinct from Paul, who in Marcion's eyes was the only faithful apostle. Thus anything even in Paul's epistles which seemed to recognize the authority of the God of Israel or to identify Him with the God and Father of our

Lord Jesus Christ was cut out; it could not, on Marcion's premises, be genuine. All Old Testament references were likewise excised."[8]

Second, many Eastern churches had begun to use in their services books whose authority was questionable. Finally, there came a time when, for practical reasons, it was crucial that serious thought be given to the canonicity of certain books. The Edict of Diocletian (A.D. 303) decreed the destruction of the sacred books of the Christians. Simply stated, what would one defend with his or her life? These people needed to know.

As was the case with the Old Testament, much debate ensued through the years with regard to the status of particular books in the New Testament. Origen devised his own canon, made up of his "acknowledged" and his "disputed" books. His disputed books consisted of 2 John, 3 John, 2 Peter, Jude, and two apocryphal works, the Letter of Barnabas and the Shepherd of Hermas.[9] Others quarreled over Hebrews, James, and Revelation. Even during the Reformation, Martin Luther spoke of a canon within a canon, evidencing his own discomfort, for example, with James, which he called "the epistle of straw." On the whole, however, most scholars agree that the canon of our present New Testament was fixed by the end of the fourth century.

EVALUATING THE CANON

The establishment of the biblical canon was a singularly important moment for the Christian church. When Athanasius mentioned his list of twenty-seven New Testament books in his Festal Letter in A.D. 367, and when that list (the same books we accept today) was for the most part agreed upon, there was in place a rule, a standard, a measure against which competing ideas, doctrinal debris, and apocryphal and pseudepigraphal works could be detected and discerned. Those charged to teach the gospel of Jesus Christ were in agreement. Those authorized to oversee doctrinal purity had a means for determining false Christs, false prophets, and false systems of salvation. The four Gospels, for example, had a quality, a message, and a feel all their own. There was a dignity, a restraint, a measure of sacred silence in the canonical works that was often missing from others claiming authenticity. Too many writings outside the canon sought to titillate the reader, to say more than they ought, to fill in the gaps, even to "lie for God" when it seemed necessary.[10] And so for a season the established canon did much to ensure doctrinal orthodoxy from branch to branch and from country to country as the Christian movement expanded its ranks.

On the other hand, an overreliance on the canon can shut one off from new truths or new insights; in addition, it can breed a sense of spiritual complacency, such that scripture readers assume that because the matter under consideration is not dealt with directly, there is no answer or God really does not care which way a given issue is settled. Further, it is ever so easy to allow oneself to slip into a form of bibliolatry in which we confuse means with ends and almost resort to scripture worship. As Elder Dallin H. Oaks declared, "What makes us different from most other Christians in the way we read and use the Bible and other scriptures is our belief in continuing revelation. For us, the scriptures are not the ultimate source of knowledge, but what precedes the ultimate source. *The ultimate knowledge comes by revelation.*"[11]

Often I encounter religious persons who state emphatically that their position is based entirely upon the authority of scripture. The truth is, God is the source of any reputable religious authority. N. T. Wright, bishop of Durham and New Testament scholar, declared: "The risen Jesus, at the end of Matthew's gospel, does not say, 'All authority in heaven and on earth is given to the books you are all going to write,' but 'All authority in heaven and on earth is given to me.'" In other words, "scripture itself points—authoritatively, if it does indeed possess authority!—away from itself and to the fact that final and true authority belongs to God himself, now delegated to Jesus Christ."[12]

Lee M. McDonald, a Baptist pastor who has taught at Fuller Theological Seminary, asks some probing questions about the present closed canon of Christian scripture. "The first question," he writes, "and the most important one, is whether the church was right in perceiving the need for a closed canon of scriptures." He asks: "Did such a move toward a closed canon of scriptures ultimately (and unconsciously) limit the presence and power of the Holy Spirit in the church? More precisely, does the recognition of absoluteness of the biblical canon minimize the presence and activity of God in the church today? . . . On what biblical or historical grounds has the inspiration of God been limited to the written documents that the church now calls its Bible?" Pastor McDonald raises other issues, but the following is his concluding: "If the Spirit inspired only the written documents of the first century, does that mean that the same Spirit does not speak today in the church about matters that are of significant concern . . . ?"[13]

I have my own questions to pose alongside those of Pastor McDonald:

1. Who authorized the canon to be closed? Does not such a move inhibit one's search for new truth, block one's openness to a later revelation from God, and, in essence, cause one to be hardened and shut off from subsequent divine illumination? Nephi warned: "Therefore, wo be unto him that is at ease in Zion! Wo be unto him that crieth: All is well! . . . Yea, wo be unto him that saith: We have received and we need no more! And in fine, wo unto all those who tremble, and are angry because of the truth of God! For behold, he that is built upon the rock receiveth it with gladness" (2 Nephi 28:24–25, 27–28).

2. Who decided that the Bible was and forevermore would be

the final written word of God? Why would one suppose that the closing words of the Apocalypse represented the "end of the prophets"?

3. Do we as Latter-day Saints not find ourselves today in a position hauntingly reminiscent of that of the early Christians relative to the continuing and ongoing mind and will of God? Is not ours the same message that Jesus and Peter and Paul and John delivered to the unbelieving Jews of their day—that the heavens had once again been opened, that new light and knowledge had burst upon the earth, and that God had chosen to reveal himself through the ministry of his Beloved Son and the Master's ordained apostles?

The truth is that no branch of Christianity limits itself entirely to the biblical text alone in making doctrinal decisions and in applying biblical principles. Roman Catholics turn to scripture, to church tradition, and to the magesterium for answers. Protestants, particularly Evangelicals, turn to linguists and scripture scholars for their answers, as well as to post–New Testament church councils and creeds. This practice seems, at least in my view, to violate *sola scriptura,* the clarion call of the Reformation to rely solely upon scripture itself. In truth there is no final authority on scriptural interpretation when differences arise, which of course they do.

The Bible is a magnificent tool in the hands of God, but it is too often used as a club or a weapon in the hands of men and women. For a long time now, the Bible has been used to settle disputes of every imaginable kind, even those that the prophets never intended to settle. Creeds and biblical interpretations in the nineteenth century served as much to distinguish and divide as they did to inform and unite. "At some level, Joseph's revelations indicate a loss of trust in the Christian ministry," LDS historian Richard Bushman has pointed out. "For all their learning and their eloquence, the clergy could not be trusted with the Bible. They did not understand what the book meant. *It was a record of revelations, and the ministry had turned it into a handbook. The Bible had become a text to be interpreted rather than an experience to be lived. In the process, the power of the book was lost.* . . . It was the power thereof that Joseph and the other visionaries of his time sought to recover. Not getting it from the ministry, they looked for it themselves.

"To me," Bushman continues, "that is Joseph Smith's significance for our time. He stood on the contested ground where the Enlightenment and Christianity confronted one another, and *his life posed the question, Do you believe God speaks?* Joseph was swept aside, of course, in the rush of ensuing intellectual battles and was disregarded by the champions of both great systems, but *his mission was to hold out for the reality of divine revelation and establish one small outpost where that principle survived.* Joseph's revelatory principle is not a single revelation serving for all time, as the Christians of his day believed regarding the incarnation of Christ, nor a mild sort of inspiration seeping into the minds of all good people, but specific, ongoing directions from God to his people. At a time when the origins of Christianity were under assault by the forces of Enlightenment rationality, Joseph Smith returned modern Christianity to its origins in revelation."[14]

ATTITUDES TOWARD THE CANON

Friends of mine, persons of other faiths who hold tenaciously to a concept of biblical sufficiency, often say to me: "But doesn't the Latter-day Saints' acceptance of the Book of Mormon and other books of scripture dilute your confidence in the Bible? Aren't you less prone to trust it, rely upon it, and turn to it when searching out doctrinal answers or personal spiritual direction? Don't you place your 'Restoration scriptures' on a higher plane than the Holy Bible?" These are penetrating questions that deserve thoughtful answers.

The Bible is one of the books within our canon of scripture, our standard works. It is fundamental and foundational. The Book of Mormon assumes that the reader already has some familiarity with the Bible, particularly as its writers address themselves to the coming of the Messiah and the destiny of the house of Israel. The Doctrine and Covenants contains revelations given to Joseph Smith and his successors, the revelations themselves often filled with biblical language and allusions. The book of Moses is Joseph Smith's inspired translation of the early chapters of Genesis. The book of Abraham is the result of Joseph Smith's translation of Egyptian papyri containing additional details about the beloved father of the faithful. Perhaps everyone has a favorite book of scripture, but all four books of holy writ are part of the royal family of scripture. We love them all. We use them all. We read and study and ponder upon each one. We cross-reference from one book of scripture to another because we are persuaded that the greatest commentary on scripture is scripture itself. And we learn from each one lessons that are both timely and timeless.

Elder M. Russell Ballard of the Quorum of the Twelve Apostles declared: "Brothers and sisters, I am sure many of you have had the experience of hearing people say that 'Mormons are not Christians because they have their own Bible, the Book of Mormon.' To anyone harboring this misconception, we say that we believe in the Lord Jesus Christ as our Savior and the author of our salvation and that we believe, revere, and love the Holy Bible. We do have additional sacred scripture, including the Book of Mormon, but it supports the Bible, never substituting for it. . . .

"Members of The Church of Jesus Christ of Latter-day Saints believe that 'all scripture is given by inspiration of God, and is profitable' (2 Timothy 3:16). We love the Bible and other scriptures. That may be surprising to some who may not be aware of our belief in the Bible as the revealed word of God. It is one of the pillars of our faith, a powerful witness of the Savior and of Christ's ongoing influence in the lives of those who worship and follow Him. The more we read and study the Bible and its teachings, the more clearly we see the doctrinal underpinnings of the restored gospel of Jesus Christ. We tend to love the scriptures that we spend time with. We may need to balance our study in order to love and understand all scripture.

"You young people especially, do not discount or devalue the Holy Bible. It is the sacred, holy record of the Lord's life. The Bible contains hundreds of pages more than all of our other scripture combined. It is the bedrock of all Christianity. We do not criticize or belittle anyone's beliefs. Our great responsibility as Christians is to share all that God has revealed with all of His sons and daughters.

"Those who join this Church do not give up their faith in the Bible—they strengthen it. The Book of Mormon does not dilute nor diminish nor de-emphasize the Bible. On the contrary, it expands, extends, and exalts it. The Book of Mormon testifies of the Bible, and both testify of Christ. . . .

"Each of these three testaments [Old Testament, New Testament, Book of Mormon] is a part of the great, indivisible whole of the Lord's revealed word to His children. They contain the words of Christ, which we have been admonished to feast upon as a means of qualifying for eternal life (see 2 Nephi 31:20). Those who think that one part is more important or more true than the other parts are missing some of the beauty and completeness of the canon of ancient scripture."[15]

In a revelation received in February 1831 that embraces "the law of the Church," the early Saints were instructed: "The elders, priests, and teachers of this church shall teach the principles of my gospel, which are *in the Bible and the Book of Mormon, in the which is the fulness of the gospel*" (D&C 42:12; emphasis added). In 1982

Elder Bruce R. McConkie explained to Church leaders that "before we can write the gospel in our own book of life we must learn the gospel as it is written in the books of scripture. The Bible, the Book of Mormon, and the Doctrine and Covenants—*each of them individually and all of them collectively—contain the fulness of the everlasting gospel.*"[16] Though Latter-day Saints do not believe that one can derive divine authority from the scriptures to perform the saving ordinances, we do say that the Bible contains the fulness of the gospel in that it teaches of groups of people in the past who enjoyed the full blessings of the everlasting gospel, and it (especially the New Testament) teaches the nature of fallen man and the good news or glad tidings of redemption in Christ through the Atonement (see 3 Nephi 27:13–21; D&C 76:40–42).

It is true that we have been taught to read the Bible through the lens of Restoration scriptures, but Christians have likewise been taught to read the Old Testament through the lens of the New Testament. Although most Christians would likely prefer to read the Gospel of John and would certainly know the life of Christ and the writings of his apostles better than they know Leviticus or 2 Chronicles or Habakkuk, yet they would quickly confess a love and respect for the entire Bible. And so it is with the Latter-day Saints. The Prophet Joseph Smith himself observed, relative to the Bible, that if we are spiritually attentive we can "see God's own handwriting in the sacred volume: and he who reads it oftenest will like it best, and he who is acquainted with it, will know the [divine] hand whenever he can see it."[17]

President Gordon B. Hinckley counseled the Saints: "I promise you that if you will read the words of that writing which we call scripture, there will come into your heart an understanding and a warmth that will be pleasing to experience. . . . Read, for instance, the Gospel of John from its beginning to its end. Let the Lord speak for himself to you, and the words will come with a quiet conviction that will make the words of his critics meaningless."[18]

One final matter. It is true that we rely heavily upon the standard works. We look to them for interpretation, for direction, and for guidance. President Joseph Fielding Smith stated: "The Bible, Book of Mormon, Doctrine and Covenants, and the Pearl of Great Price, including the Articles of Faith, have been received by the vote of the Church in general conference assembled as the standard works of the Church. On this platform we stand. . . .

"If I should say something which is contrary to that which is written and approved by the Church generally, no one is under obligation to accept it. Everything that I say and everything that any other person says must square itself with that which the Lord has revealed, or it should be rejected."[19]

And yet we speak of the restored church as a "living church" (D&C 1:30), one open and attentive to the Lord's inspiration, prophetic clarification, and even supplementation of the canon. I sat in general conference in April 1976 when the record of two visions—Joseph Smith's vision of the celestial kingdom (D&C 137) and Joseph F. Smith's vision of the redemption of the dead (D&C 138)—were added to the canon of scripture by a sustaining vote of the assembled Saints. In that action and on that day, these two visions, both true and instructive and inspired from the day they were received, changed in status: they moved from *scripture*—that which is given by the power of the Spirit and represents the will, mind, word, and voice of the Almighty (D&C 68:4)—to *canonized scripture.* They thereby became binding upon the Saints as a body. Wise teachers and gospel students had read and taught from them before, but now *all* Saints were expected to conform their study, their teaching, and their lives with the doctrine set forth within them.

Further, because we are a living Church and because such additions to the standard works do not take place very often (in 1976 it had been almost a century since revelations had been added), we look to the living apostles and prophets, the living oracles, for living fruit from the living tree of life, even if such enlightenment is not within the canon. Such vital doctrinal expositions as "The Origin of Man" (1909) and "The Father and the Son" (1916) guide our study and inform our interpretation of scripture, but they have not been added to the canon. Such magnificent presentations as "The Family: A Proclamation to the World" (1995) and "The Living Christ" (2000) are like manna to the soul and as steel reinforcers in our houses of faith, but they are not in the canon. So although we look regularly and consistently to the standard works in ascertaining gospel truth, we remain open to the precious and prophesied flood of light that we know as the restitution of all things (Acts 3:21).

CONCLUSION

Surely nothing is more set, fixed, and established than the truth that the canon of scripture is open, flexible, and expanding. Truly, we believe that God "will yet reveal many great and important things pertaining to the kingdom of God" (Article of Faith 9). We have not received the final word. There is much, much more to come, as the scriptures of the Restoration attest. Elder Neal A. Maxwell once wrote that "today we carry convenient quadruple combinations of the scriptures, but one day, since more scriptures are coming, we may need to pull little red wagons brim with books."[20]

"There are those who would assume that with the printing and binding of these sacred records, that would be the 'end of the prophets,'" President Spencer W. Kimball declared. "But again we testify to the world that revelation continues and that the vaults and files of the Church contain these revelations which come month to month and day to day."[21]

Our God speaks. He will not be silenced. He will not fail to reveal his mind and will to his children as they continue to importune him for revelation, both individually and institutionally. That righteousness and truth may continue to rain down from heaven and that we may treasure up the holy word is my earnest prayer.

CHAPTER TWELVE

A PERSONAL WITNESS

I think I have always had a testimony. I don't know of a time when I didn't believe in God, inasmuch as Mom and Dad taught me to kneel beside my bed and offer a simple prayer when I was very young. Even during the time when we were not particularly active in the Church, especially when we lived in Nashville, Tennessee (where I started school), Mom enrolled me in a vacation Bible school, where I was taught much about Jesus. I believed what I was taught, and I was always moved by the stories of the Master's ministry. I felt that the stories were true, that they really had happened. When we returned to the Church, at about the time I was baptized, I began paying closer attention to members of our Baton Rouge ward who spoke in sacrament meeting or taught lessons, especially those who bore their testimony during the monthly fast and testimony meeting. I was moved by their sincerity, but there was more to it than that; I was touched and stimulated by the words they spoke and the conviction they expressed. They would use such phrases as "I know that this gospel is true" or "I have a testimony that Jesus Christ is the Son of the Living God" or "I know that Joseph Smith was a prophet of God" or "I know that

President David O. McKay is God's prophet on the earth today" or "I know that this Church is true." I didn't understand all they said, but I sensed that such declarations were part and parcel of their very makeup, that what they believed, what they knew, was central to who they were and how they lived.

Acquiring a testimony of the gospel of Jesus Christ is a remarkable thing. It is a miracle, an instance in which the Infinite affects the finite, in which the heavens touch the earth, in which Spirit speaks to spirit, in which God manifests truth to mortals. To gain a testimony is to be reborn to what we know and feel and value (1 John 5:1). One who has received such a manifestation is a new creature, a new creature in Christ. "To know God our Eternal Father and Jesus Christ, whom he sent," President Marion G. Romney explained, "one must, as did the Apostles of old, learn of them through the process of divine revelation. One must be born again."[1]

FACING HARD QUESTIONS

A testimony of the gospel of Jesus Christ is and must be a living, growing, expanding, and deepening phenomenon. President Harold B. Lee explained to a group of full-time missionaries in my mission that a testimony is as delicate as an orchid, as elusive as a moonbeam; our testimonies today will not necessarily be our testimonies tomorrow. We must study and ponder and pray and serve and forsake ungodliness if we are to retain our faith, our witness of the truth. It has been just so with me. Some things that I came to know at age eight, by the power of the Spirit, I knew more fervently at age eighteen. Some doctrinal matters that made pretty good sense to me at twenty now make perfect sense at sixty.

It has been my interesting but unpleasant opportunity over the past three decades to engage firsthand with a great deal of anti-Mormon propaganda. I am, to be sure, absolutely stunned that men and women who claim to be Christian can waste and wear out their lives seeking to tear down what they cannot understand, doing so with a venom and a horrid bitterness that is anything but Christian. I receive scores of letters and e-mails and view a surprising number of video presentations prepared by critics and scoffers who claim to have the sure word, the only correct and penetrating insight into The Church of Jesus Christ of Latter-day Saints. I seldom respond, for it is clear that the last thing such persons really want is an answer to their questions.

Nonetheless, one e-mail I received a few years ago was so filled with hatred and animosity that I felt I simply must respond. I wrote: "Is there not anything you stand *for?* It is abundantly clear to anyone who knows you or your work what you are *against,* but it seems a terrible tragedy to go to your grave having spent your days seeking to destroy the religious lives of other human beings, who have just as much right in this country to their private beliefs as you do. If we as Latter-day Saints are not Christian, as you contend, and if in fact you *are* Christian, and your language and behavior and manner of communicating represent the best Christianity has to offer, I would simply ask, Who in their right mind would ever want to be a Christian?"

I do not have the answers to all the questions raised by our critics. Some things simply have not been made known to us. For the time being I figuratively place them on the shelf. I am not ashamed to admit that I have placed many things on the shelf over the years, nor do I hesitate to point out that many of those items have been removed from the shelf as my gospel understanding and maturity have deepened. My attitude is quite simple: I refuse to allow things that I do not know to unsettle or tarnish that which I *do* know.

Let me explain further how I deal with matters, especially sensitive matters, to which I cannot provide either a satisfactory or a soothing answer. Let's take the life of Jesus Christ. We know that he lived a perfect life, that he never took a moral detour or a backward step. These things are attested in scripture (see 2 Corinthians 5:21; Hebrews 4:15; 1 Peter 2:22; JST Hebrews 7:26). Therefore, anytime something in the New Testament is said or done by the Savior that seems a bit unusual or unkind or even mean-spirited, I reason this way: Jesus was and is the Son of God. He lived a perfect life and is rightfully known as the sinless Son of Man. Having that knowledge as my foundation, I choose to view everything the Master does through the lens of his perfection. Thus, if his comment to his mother at the wedding of Cana (see John 2:4) appears a little short or abrupt, I know (even without the assistance of the Joseph Smith Translation) that he did not intend to be unkind or disrespectful to one he dearly loved.

A colleague at Brigham Young University shared an experience that highlights this principle. His New Testament class had come to a study of John 7–10, where the Lord is quite straightforward with the Pharisees and scribes.

One young student raised a hand. "This section bothers me. I think Jesus' comments are unchristian."

Startled, my colleague responded, "Would you repeat that?"

The student shot back, "Well, I think Jesus is being very unChristlike here."

My colleague asked, "Is that possible? Jesus himself is the standard against which we judge goodness and especially Christlikeness. How can Christ be unchristian?"

I deal with sensitive questions involving the Prophet Joseph Smith and the Restoration in a similar way. When someone confronts me with a hard question about the practice of plural marriage, for example, I explain what I do understand and then say, essentially, "I have a testimony and a witness, deep within my soul, that Joseph Smith was called of God—that the First Vision actually took place, that the Book of Mormon was translated by the gift and power of God, that angels appeared and restored priest-hood keys, and that revelations concerning doctrine and practice came through him to the Latter-day Saints and the world. These things I know. I have read and studied and prayed about them, and God has answered my prayers. I do not understand everything about the practice of plural marriage, but this much I do know: Joseph Smith was God's covenant spokesman, the head of this final gospel dispensation. One day we will come to understand things better. In the meantime, I choose not to be troubled or confused but rather to give the Prophet Joseph the benefit of the doubt."

WHY I AM A LATTER-DAY SAINT

I have sat in huge cathedrals around the world and witnessed the quiet, steady devotion of their congregants. I have attended worship services in tiny church houses with persons who read their Bibles and pray with great fervency. I have had long and pen-etrating conversations with some of the most informed and intelli-gent men and women in the world, churchmen and professors of religion, whose commitment to their tradition is deep and poignant and exemplary. I have heard gospel truth preached in other houses of worship, and I have felt the quiet assurance that God was pleased with what was taking place. Now, although I am eager to love my brothers and sisters of all faiths, I do believe that the ful-ness of salvation comes only in and through the name and work of Jesus the Christ (Acts 4:12; Mosiah 3:17) and that the only ulti-mate solution to this world's ills, including the proliferation of ter-rorism and war, is to be found in Christianity.

I am first and foremost a son of God. I am a Christian. I am a Latter-day Saint. I am part of the larger body of Christ. I have read hundreds of books and articles setting forth the beliefs and prac-tices of other churches, and there is a great deal that interests and intrigues me. My to-read pile is still quite healthy, and I have every intention of doing all I can before I die to better understand those who have chosen other religious persuasions. At the same time, I have never been more convinced than I am right now that The Church of Jesus Christ of Latter-day Saints has a distinctive contribution to make to the world, a unique voice to be heard at the religious roundtable, and singular insights to be offered to honest seekers of truth regarding our lives before we were born, the purposes of life here, and the nature of life hereafter. Latter-day Saints have principles to teach concerning God's eternal plan for the family that would revolutionize how people view marriage and children and how such principles operate to bring peace and security and healing into troubled homes and hearts.

I am a Latter-day Saint because I believe in God the Eternal Father. I am a Latter-day Saint because I believe in the divine Sonship of Jesus Christ. I am a Latter-day Saint because I believe in the truthfulness of the Bible. I am a Latter-day Saint because I believe that sins are forgiven, hearts transformed, natures changed, and the dead resurrected through the infinite and eternal atoning sacrifice of Christ. I am a Latter-day Saint because I believe that God called upon Joseph Smith to restore priesthood authority and many plain and precious truths that had been lost. I am a Latter-day Saint because I believe that the keys of the kingdom of God have come down in rightful succession (by the laying on of hands) from Joseph Smith to the present day. I am a Latter-day Saint because I believe the Book of Mormon is the word of God: it feeds my soul just as the Bible does; reading 2 Nephi lifts my spirits as much as reading the Gospel of John. I know holy scripture when I read it.

I am a Latter-day Saint because I know these things to be true, know them in a manner as powerful as that I know I live. I have not invested my life in a religious enterprise just because of some emotional attachment to lofty ideas, some warm and fuzzy feeling, but rather as a result of a divine investiture to me of eternal truth, saving and sanctifying truth. I have not chosen to cast my lot with the Mormons simply because I like being with the people (although I do enjoy sociality with the Saints immensely), but rather because the Spirit of the Living God has graced me with a witness that burns like fire within my soul, a witness from God Almighty that affirms that what those Mormons are about is right and true and good. I am willing to give my life for that witness, and I am willing to go to my death, if need be, as a sign of gratitude and love to a gracious and truth-revealing God. I am a Latter-day Saint, in short, because the sacred work in which I spend my time, energy, and resources is a work that is ongoing, expansive, and everlasting. It is the true and living work of our Savior Jesus Christ.

NOTES

Introduction
LAYING THE DOCTRINAL FOUNDATION

1. McConkie, *Doctrines of the Restoration,* 226–27.

2. *Teachings of the Prophet Joseph Smith,* 274.

3. *Teachings of the Prophet Joseph Smith,* 319.

4. Hinckley, Conference Report, October 1998, 90; emphasis added.

5. Packer, Conference Report, October 1986, 20; see also "Do Not Fear," *Ensign,* May 2004, 79; McConkie, *New Witness for the Articles of Faith,* 699–700.

6. Maxwell, *One More Strain of Praise,* x.

7. Hinckley, "Symbol of Our Membership," *Ensign*, April 2005, 2–6.

8. Interview with Don Lattin, a reporter in San Jose, California; emphasis added.

9. Hinckley, Conference Report, October 1996, 71.

Chapter One
IN THE SPRING OF 1820

1. Adapted from Backman, *American Religions and the Rise of Mormonism,* Appendix D.

2. See Backman, *Joseph Smith's First Vision,* chap. 3.

3. See Madsen, *Joseph Smith the Prophet*, 8; McConkie, *New Witness for the Articles of Faith*, 5.

4. McConkie, *New Witness for the Articles of Faith*, 5.

5. See Backman, *Joseph Smith's First Vision*, 155–69.

6. Cited in Backman, *Joseph Smith's First Vision*, 158–59; spelling and punctuation standardized.

7. From Backman, *Joseph Smith's First Vision*, 172.

8. From Backman, *Joseph Smith's First Vision*, 169.

9. *Teachings of the Prophet Joseph Smith*, 347.

10. *Teachings of the Prophet Joseph Smith*, 367.

11. From Backman, *Joseph Smith's First Vision*, 157; punctuation, spelling, and capitalization standardized.

12. *Teachings of the Prophet Joseph Smith*, 370.

13. See Milton V. Backman Jr., "Truman Coe's 1836 Description of Mormonism," *Brigham Young University Studies* 17, no. 3 (Spring 1977), 354.

14. *Words of Joseph Smith*, 60.

15. *Words of Joseph Smith*, 64.

16. Smith, *Doctrines of Salvation*, 1:28.

17. *History of the Church*, 4:536.

18. Letter of 6 June 1832, in *Personal Writings of Joseph Smith*, 264–65; punctuation standardized.

19. *Teachings of the Prophet Joseph Smith*, 157.

20. McConkie, "This Generation Shall Have My Word through You," in *Hearken, O Ye People*, 4.

21. McConkie, "This Generation Shall Have My Word through You," in *Hearken, O Ye People*, 4–5.

22. Smith, *Gospel Doctrine*, 495.

23. Cannon, *Life of Joseph Smith the Prophet*, 31–32.

24. Pratt, *Journal of Discourses*, 12:354.

25. *Teachings of Spencer W. Kimball*, 430.

26. *Teachings of Gordon B. Hinckley*, 236.

Chapter Two
SETTING THE KEYSTONE

1. *History of the Church,* 4:461.

2. *History of the Church,* 4:461; see also *Teachings of the Prophet Joseph Smith,* 194.

3. Webster, *American Dictionary of the English Language,* s.v. "correct."

4. *New Shorter Oxford English Dictionary,* s.v. "correct."

5. See *Teachings of the Prophet Joseph Smith,* 9–10, 61, 327.

6. Hinckley, Conference Report, April 1966.

7. LDS Student Association fireside, Utah State University, 10 October 1971.

8. Holland, Conference Report, October 2003, 73–75.

9. Holland, *Christ and the New Covenant,* 345.

10. Benson, *Witness and a Warning,* 18.

11. Benson, *Witness and a Warning,* 18.

12. Benson, *Witness and a Warning,* 18–19.

13. Benson, *Witness and a Warning,* 19.

14. Holland, *Christ and the New Covenant,* 345.

15. Holland, *Christ and the New Covenant,* 345–46.

16. Webster, *American Dictionary of the English Language,* s.v. "precept."

17. *New Shorter Oxford English Dictionary,* s.v. "precept."

18. Holland, *Christ and the New Covenant,* 347, 349.

19. Benson, *Witness and a Warning,* 13.

20. Benson, *Witness and a Warning,* 19–20; emphasis added.

21. Benson, *Witness and a Warning,* 10, 21–22.

22. McConkie, Conference Report, April 1982, 50.

23. McConkie, Conference Report, October 1983, 105–6.

24. Benson, *Witness and a Warning,* 7–8.

25. Benson, Conference Report, October 1988, 4–5.

26. *Messenger and Advocate* 2 (October 1835): 199.

27. *Teachings of Gordon B. Hinckley,* 38.

Chapter Three
LIVING DOCTRINE

1. *Teachings of the Prophet Joseph Smith,* 121.

2. Packer, Conference Report, April 1977, 80; emphasis added.

3. *Teachings of Gordon B. Hinckley,* 620.

4. *Teachings of the Prophet Joseph Smith,* 392.

5. Smith, *Gospel Doctrine,* 9.

6. Retrieved from ldschurch.org, "Newsroom," 4 May 2007.

7. Compare *Teachings of the Prophet Joseph Smith,* 9–10, 61, 327.

8. *Teachings of the Prophet Joseph Smith,* 278.

9. *Teachings of the Prophet Joseph Smith,* 268.

10. As cited in Maxwell, Conference Report, October 1984, 10.

11. McKay, Conference Report, April 1907, 11–12; see also October 1912, 121; April 1962, 7.

12. *Teachings of the Prophet Joseph Smith,* 89.

13. Hinckley, Conference Report, April 1992, 77.

14. Hinckley, "The Continuous Pursuit of Truth," *Ensign,* April 1986, 5.

15. Oaks, *Provo Daily Herald,* 5 June 1988, 21.

16. First Presidency letter [David O. McKay, Hugh B. Brown, and N. Eldon Tanner], January 1970.

17. McConkie, "The New Revelation on Priesthood," in *Priesthood,* 132.

18. *Teachings of the Prophet Joseph Smith,* 345–46.

19. *Teachings of Lorenzo Snow,* 1.

20. Smith, *Lectures on Faith,* 2:2.

21. "Editor's Table," *Improvement Era* 15 (September 1912): 1042.

22. *Teachings of Harold B. Lee,* 157.

23. Maxwell, *Men and Women of Christ,* 2.

24. Personal correspondence to Robert J. Matthews, 28 January 1969; cited in Matthews, "Using the Scriptures," *BYU Fireside and Devotional Speeches, 1981,* 124.

25. Maxwell, *That My Family Should Partake,* 87.

26. Maxwell, *All These Things Shall Give Thee Experience,* 4.

Chapter Four
CHRIST'S ETERNAL GOSPEL

1. McConkie, *Promised Messiah*, 4–5.

2. *Teachings of the Prophet Joseph Smith*, 59–60.

3. *Teachings of the Prophet Joseph Smith*, 264.

4. *Teachings of the Prophet Joseph Smith*, 168.

5. *Teachings of the Prophet Joseph Smith*, 308.

6. Smith, *Doctrines of Salvation*, 1:156.

7. Roberts, *Defense of the Faith and the Saints*, 1:512–13.

8. Smith, *Gospel Doctrine*, 30, 395, 398–400; see also *Journal of Discourses*, 15:325.

9. Nibley, *Message of the Joseph Smith Papyri*, xii-xiii.

10. Young, *Journal of Discourses*, 2:139.

11. See D&C 84:46–48; Smith, *Gospel Doctrine*, 67–68; McConkie, *New Witness for the Articles of Faith*, 260–61.

12. Smith, *Gospel Doctrine*, 13.

Chapter Five
THE INFINITE AND INTIMATE ATONEMENT

1. *Teachings of the Prophet Joseph Smith*, 121.

2. Lewis, *Mere Christianity*, 51–52.

3. *Times and Seasons* 4 (1 February 1843): 82–83.

4. Nelson, *Perfection Pending*, 167.

5. Lewis, *Mere Christianity*, 168.

6. Bateman, Conference Report, October 2005, 77.

7. Maxwell, *Even As I Am*, 116–17.

8. Holland, *Trusting Jesus*, 68.

9. Lewis, *Mere Christianity*, 146–47.

10. *Teachings of Gordon B. Hinckley*, 28.

Chapter Six
WHAT HAPPENED TO THE CROSS?

1. McConkie, Conference Report, April 1985, 11.

2. Holland, *Trusting Jesus,* 35.

3. MacArthur, *Hard to Believe,* 26–27.

4. Hengel, *Crucifixion in the Ancient World* (Philadelphia: Fortress Press, 1977), 6–7, as cited in MacArthur, *Hard to Believe,* 29.

5. *Gospel Doctrine,* 91; emphasis added.

6. Young, *Journal of Discourses,* 13:56.

7. Davies, *Private Passions,* 77–87.

8. See Ehrman, *Orthodox Corruption of Scripture,* 94; Metzger, *Textual Commentary on the Greek New Testament,* 151.

9. Young, *Journal of Discourses,* 3:205–6.

10. Taylor, *Gospel Kingdom,* 114.

11. Woodruff, Smith, and Thatcher, *Contributor* 9 (June 1888), no. 8.

12. See Clark, *Messages of the First Presidency,* 5:208.

13. Roberts, *Seventy's Course in Theology,* vol. 4.

14. Wirthlin, Conference Report, October 1952, 108.

15. McConkie, Conference Report, April 1985, 10; emphasis added; compare *Mortal Messiah,* 4:230; *New Witness for the Articles of Faith,* 620; see also Talmage, *Jesus the Christ,* 613, 660–61.

16. *Teachings of Ezra Taft Benson,* 14.

17. Hinckley, Christmas devotional, 8 December 1996, as cited in *Church News,* 14 December 1996, 2; see also *Church News,* 3 September 2005, 2.

18. Hinckley, "The Symbol of Our Faith," *Ensign,* April 2005, 4.

19. Hinckley, Regional Conference, St. George, Utah, 24 November 2002, as cited in *Church News,* 5 November 2005, 2.

20. *Hymns,* ix-x; emphasis added.

21. Packer, Conference Report, October 1985, 107; emphasis in original.

22. Young, *Journal of Discourses* 12:33–34; emphasis added.

23. *History of the Church,* 4:78.

24. *Teachings of the Prophet Joseph Smith,* 121.

Chapter Seven

THE GREATEST GIFT

1. Pratt, *True Faith,* 3–9; see also *Orson Pratt's Works,* 51.

2. Lewis, *Mere Christianity,* 165.

3. Benson, Conference Report, October 1985, 5–6.

4. MacArthur, *Faith Works,* 32.

5. Packer, Conference Report, October 1995, 23.

6. Young, *Journal of Discourses,* 4:91.

7. Young, *Journal of Discourses,* 3:155.

8. Lewis, *Mere Christianity,* 131–32.

9. Bonhoeffer, *Cost of Discipleship,* 47–48.

Chapter Eight
BEYOND THE VEIL

1. *Teachings of the Prophet Joseph Smith,* 324.

2. *Diary of Charles L. Walker,* 1:595–96; emphasis added; spelling and punctuation standardized.

3. Smith, address given at the funeral of Elder Richard L. Evans, 4 November 1971, 2; see also Kimball, *Faith Precedes the Miracle,* 103, 105.

4. *Teachings of the Prophet Joseph Smith,* 326.

5. *Teachings of the Prophet Joseph Smith,* 196–97.

6. Young, *Journal of Discourses,* 14:231.

7. Pratt, *Journal of Discourses,* 2:243, 246.

8. *Teachings of the Prophet Joseph Smith,* 56.

9. *History of the Church,* 1:341.

10. *Teachings of the Prophet Joseph Smith,* 326; emphasis added.

11. Young, *Journal of Discourses,* 3:372.

12. Pratt, *Key to the Science of Theology,* 80.

13. Smith, *Gospel Doctrine,* 448–49.

14. Smith, *Gospel Doctrine,* 448.

15. Pratt, *Journal of Discourses,* 1:289.

16. Young, *Journal of Discourses,* 3:95; emphasis added.

17. *Teachings of the Prophet Joseph Smith,* 310.

18. *Teachings of the Prophet Joseph Smith,* 367.

19. Smith, *Doctrines of Salvation,* 2:158, 230.

20. Packer, Conference Report, April 1992, 94.

21. Woodruff, as cited in Packer, *Holy Temple,* 206.

22. Snow, Conference Report, October 1893; or *Collected Discourses,* 3:363; emphasis added.

23. Smith, *Gospel Doctrine,* 448.

24. *Teachings of the Prophet Joseph Smith,* 62.

25. *Teachings of the Prophet Joseph Smith,* 199–200.

26. Smith, *Gospel Doctrine,* 23.

27. *History of the Church,* 5:339.

28. "The Resurrection" [1875], *Elders' Journal* 1 (July 1904): 153.

29. Smith, *Gospel Doctrine,* 25.

30. *Teachings of the Prophet Joseph Smith,* 296.

31. *Teachings of the Prophet Joseph Smith,* 296.

Chapter Nine
GOD AND HUMAN TRAGEDY

1. Stackhouse, *Can God Be Trusted?* 2.

2. Kimball, *Faith Precedes the Miracle,* 96.

3. Smith, *Lectures on Faith,* 2:2.

4. Stackhouse, *Can God Be Trusted?* 73.

5. Lewis, *Problem of Pain,* 35–36.

6. Stackhouse, *Can God Be Trusted?* 13.

7. Swinburne, *Is There a God?* 99.

8. Swinburne, *Is There a God?* 98–99, 103.

9. Stackhouse, *Can God Be Trusted?* 66–67; see also Plantinga, *God and Other Minds,* 13–55.

10. Packer, *The Play and the Plan,* 2–3.

11. Maxwell, Conference Report, October 1974, 16.

12. Lewis, *Problem of Pain,* 37–38.

13. Scott, Conference Report, October 1995, 18.

14. Frankl, *Man's Search for Meaning,* 104.

15. Lewis, *Mere Christianity,* 131.

16. Hunter, Conference Report, October 1979, 93.

17. Marilyn McCord Adams, "Redemptive Suffering: A Christian Solution to the Problem of Evil," in *Rationality, Religious Belief and Moral Commitment,* ed. Robert Audi and William J. Wainwright (Ithaca, N.Y.:

Cornell University Press, 1986), as cited in Stackhouse, *Can God Be Trusted?* 175–76.

18. *Teachings of the Prophet Joseph Smith,* 220.

19. Packer, Conference Report, October 1983, 21–22.

20. *Teachings of the Prophet Joseph Smith,* 162.

21. Holland, Conference Report, October 1999, 45.

Chapter Ten
THE BLESSINGS OF THE TEMPLE

1. *Teachings of the Prophet Joseph Smith,* 121.

2. Richard Kugelman, "The First Letter to the Corinthians," in *Jerome Biblical Commentary,* 2:273.

3. Fee, *First Epistle to the Corinthians,* 767.

4. For a summary of some of the alternative explanations see Fee, *First Epistle to the Corinthians,* 763–77; see also a more recent proposal in Joel R. White, "'Baptized on Behalf of the Dead,': The Meaning of 1 Corinthians 15:29 in Its Context," *Journal of Biblical Literature* 116, 3 (1997): 487–99.

5. Richard E. DeMaris, "Corinthian Religion and Baptism for the Dead (1 Corinthians 15:29): Insights from Archaeology and Anthropology," *Journal of Biblical Literature* 114, 4 (1995): 678, 679.

6. Anderson, *Understanding Paul,* 405.

7. MacCulloch, *Harrowing of Hell,* 49.

8. MacCulloch, *Harrowing of Hell,* 84–85; see also *Ante-Nicene Fathers,* 1:235.

9. Irenaeus, *Against Heresies* 4.27.1, in Lightfoot, *Apostolic Fathers,* 277–78.

10. *The Shepherd of Hermas,* similitude 9.16.2–4; as cited in Anderson, *Understanding Paul,* 409; emphasis added.

11. Ehrman, *Lost Scriptures,* 33.

12. Goppelt, *Commentary on 1 Peter,* 263, 259.

13. *Teachings of the Prophet Joseph Smith,* 179.

14. *Teachings of the Prophet Joseph Smith,* 201.

15. Farrar, *Early Days of Christianity,* 139–42, 169.

16. *Teachings of the Prophet Joseph Smith,* 367.

17. *Teachings of the Prophet Joseph Smith,* 191.

18. Carson, *Christianity Today,* 10 August 1998, 63.

19. *Teachings of the Prophet Joseph Smith,* 307–8; emphasis added.

20. Nelson, "Thanks for the Covenant," *BYU Devotional and Fireside Speeches, 1998–99,* 89.

21. *Teachings of the Prophet Joseph Smith,* 335.

22. *Teachings of the Prophet Joseph Smith,* 158.

23. *Teachings of the Prophet Joseph Smith,* 91.

24. Matthews, *Unto All Nations,* 1–2.

25. See Nibley, *Mormonism and Early Christianity,* 10–44.

26. Smith, *Words of Joseph Smith,* 211; spelling and punctuation standardized.

27. Backman, *Heavens Resound,* 285.

28. Backman, *Heavens Resound,* 285–87.

29. See Smith, *Words of Joseph Smith,* 49.

30. See McConkie, *New Witness for the Articles of Faith,* 508.

31. Roberts, *Comprehensive History of the Church,* 1:521.

32. Maxwell, *But for a Small Moment,* 17.

33. *Deseret News Semi-Weekly,* 15 February 1884, 2.

34. *Teachings of the Prophet Joseph Smith,* 237.

35. *Teachings of the Prophet Joseph Smith,* 308.

36. *Teachings of the Prophet Joseph Smith,* 322.

37. *Teachings of the Prophet Joseph Smith,* 321.

38. *Discourses of Wilford Woodruff,* 72.

39. *Teachings of the Prophet Joseph Smith,* 191–92.

40. *Autobiography of Parley P. Pratt,* 297–98.

41. Hunter, Conference Report, October 1994, 8.

42. *Teachings of Gordon B. Hinckley,* 638.

43. McConkie, *New Witness for the Articles of Faith,* 539.

Chapter Eleven
THE LIVING CANON

1. Bruce, *Books and the Parchments,* 95.

2. Bruce, *Books and the Parchments,* 95–96.

3. Geisler and Nix, *General Introduction to the Bible,* 138–53.

4. Goodspeed, *How Came the Bible?* 23.

5. *Interpreter's Dictionary of the Bible,* s.v. "Jabneel." See also Bruce, *Books and the Parchments,* 98; Goodspeed, *How Came the Bible?* 41.

6. J. S. Wright, *Evangelical Quarterly,* April 1947, 97, as cited in Bruce, *Books and the Parchments,* 98.

7. Goodspeed, *How Came the Bible?* 49–50.

8. Bruce, *Books and the Parchments,* 108. Soon after the time of Marcion, in the last quarter of the second century, the term *New Testament* began to be used to refer to the collection of Christian scriptures, whereas *Old Testament* referred to the Jewish scriptures.

9. Goodspeed, *How Came the Bible?* 78–79.

10. See Stephen E. Robinson, "Lying for God: The Uses of Apocrypha," in *Apocryphal Writings and the Latter-day Saints,* 133–54.

11. Oaks, "Scripture Reading, Revelation, and Joseph Smith's Translation of the Bible," in *Plain and Precious Truths Restored,* 2; emphasis added.

12. Wright, *Last Word,* xi, 24.

13. McDonald, *Formation of the Christian Biblical Canon,* 254–56.

14. Bushman, "A Joseph Smith for the Twenty-first Century," *Believing History,* 274; emphasis added.

15. Ballard, "The Miracle of the Holy Bible," *Ensign,* May 2007, 81–82.

16. McConkie, "Holy Writ: Published Anew," Regional Representatives Seminar, 2 April 1982; *Doctrines of the Restoration,* 237; emphasis added.

17. *Teachings of the Prophet Joseph Smith,* 56.

18. *Teachings of Gordon B. Hinckley,* 572.

19. Smith, *Doctrines of Salvation* 1:322–23.

20. Maxwell, *Wonderful Flood of Light,* 18; see also Maxwell, "The Children of Christ," in *Mosiah: Salvation Only through Christ,* 1.

21. Kimball, Conference Report, April 1977, 115.

Chapter Twelve
A PERSONAL WITNESS

1. Romney, Conference Report, October 1981, 18–20.

SOURCES

Anderson, Richard Lloyd. *Understanding Paul.* Salt Lake City: Deseret Book, 1983.

Apocryphal Writings and the Latter-day Saints. Ed. C. Wilfred Griggs. Provo, Utah: BYU Religious Studies Center, 1986.

The Ante-Nicene Fathers: The Writings of the Fathers Down to A.D. 325. Ed. Alexander Roberts and James Donaldson. Rev. A. Cleveland Coxe. 1885–96. Reprint. Peabody, Mass.: Hendrickson Publishers, 1994.

Backman, Milton V., Jr. *American Religions and the Rise of Mormonism.* Rev. ed. Salt Lake City: Deseret Book, 1970.

———. *The Heavens Resound: A History of the Latter-day Saints in Ohio, 1830–1838.* Salt Lake City: Deseret Book, 1983.

———. *Joseph Smith's First Vision.* 2d ed. Salt Lake City: Bookcraft, 1980.

Believing History: Latter-day Saint Essays. Ed. Reid L. Neilson and Jed Woodworth. New York: Columbia University Press, 2004.

Benson, Ezra Taft. *A Witness and a Warning: A Modern-day Prophet Testifies of the Book of Mormon.* Salt Lake City: Deseret Book, 1988.

———. *The Teachings of Ezra Taft Benson.* Salt Lake City: Bookcraft, 1988.

Bercot, David W., ed. *A Dictionary of Early Christian Beliefs.* Peabody, Mass.: Hendrickson, 1998.

Bonhoeffer, Dietrich. *The Cost of Discipleship.* New York: Macmillan, 1963.

Brigham Young University Fireside and Devotional Speeches, 1981. Provo, Utah: University Publications Department, 1981.

Brigham Young University Devotional and Fireside Speeches, 1988–89. Ed. Karen Seely. Provo, Utah: University Publications Department, 1989.

Bruce, F. F. *The Books and the Parchments: Some Chapters on the Transmission of the Bible.* 3d ed. rev. Westwood, N.J.: Fleming H. Revell, 1963.

Cannon, George Q. *Gospel Truth: Discourses and Writings of George Q. Cannon.* Ed. Jerreld L. Newquist. 2 vols. in 1. Salt Lake City: Deseret Book, 1987.

———. *Life of Joseph Smith the Prophet.* Salt Lake City: Deseret Book, 1972.

Collected Discourses Delivered by President Wilford Woodruff, His Two Counselors, the Twelve Apostles, and Others. Comp. Brian Stuy. 5 vols. Sandy, Utah: B.H.S. Publishing, 1987–92.

Davies, Douglas. *Private Passions: Betraying Discipleship on the Journey to Jerusalem.* Norwich, England: Canterbury Press, 2000.

Ehrman, Bart D. *Lost Scriptures: Books That Did Not Make It into the New Testament.* New York: Oxford University Press, 2003.

———. *The Orthodox Corruption of Scripture: The Effect of Early Christological Controversies on the Text of the New Testament.* New York: Oxford University Press, 1993.

Farrar, Frederic W. *The Early Days of Christianity.* New York: Cassell, Petter, Galpin & Co., 1882.

Fee, Gordon D. *The First Epistle to the Corinthians.* Grand Rapids, Mich.: Eerdmans, 1987.

Frankl, Viktor E. *Man's Search for Meaning.* New York: Washington Square Press, 1985.

Geisler, Norman L., and William E. Nix. *A General Introduction to the Bible.* Chicago: Moody Press, 1968.

Goodspeed, Edgar J. *How Came the Bible?* New York: Abingdon Press, 1940.

Goppelt, Leonhard. *A Commentary on 1 Peter.* Ed. Ferdinand Hahn. Trans. John E. Alsup. Grand Rapids, Mich.: Eerdmans, 1993.

Hearken, O Ye People. Salt Lake City: Randall Book, 1984.

Hinckley, Gordon B. *Faith, the Essence of True Religion.* Salt Lake City: Deseret Book, 1989.

————. *Teachings of Gordon B. Hinckley.* Salt Lake City: Deseret Book, 1997.

Holland, Jeffrey R. *Christ and the New Covenant: The Messianic Message of the Book of Mormon.* Salt Lake City: Deseret Book, 1997.

————. *Trusting Jesus.* Salt Lake City: Deseret Book, 2003.

Hymns of The Church of Jesus Christ of Latter-day Saints. Salt Lake City: The Church of Jesus Christ of Latter-day Saints, 1985.

The Interpreter's Dictionary of the Bible: An Illustrated Encyclopedia. Ed. George Arthur Buttrick. 4 vols. New York: Abingdon Press, 1962.

Jerome Biblical Commentary. Ed. Raymond E. Brown, Joseph A. Fitzmyer, and Roland E. Murphy. 2 vols. Englewood Cliffs, N.J.: Prentice-Hall, 1968.

Journal of Discourses. 26 vols. Liverpool: F. D. Richards & Sons, 1851–86.

Kimball, Spencer W. *Faith Precedes the Miracle.* Salt Lake City: Deseret Book, 1974.

————. *Teachings of Spencer W. Kimball.* Ed. Edward L. Kimball. Salt Lake City: Bookcraft, 1982.

Kirkham, Francis W. *A New Witness for Christ in America.* Independence, Mo.: Zion's Printing, 1942.

Lee, Harold B. *Teachings of Harold B. Lee.* Ed. Clyde J. Williams. Salt Lake City: Bookcraft, 1996.

Lewis, C. S. *Mere Christianity.* San Francisco: Harper, 2001.

————. *The Problem of Pain.* New York: Touchstone Books, 1996.

Lightfoot, J. B. *The Apostolic Fathers.* Grand Rapids, Mich.: Baker Book House, 1962.

MacArthur, John. *Faith Works: The Gospel According to the Apostles.* Dallas: Word Publishing, 1993.

————. *Hard to Believe: The High Cost and Infinite Value of Following Jesus.* Nashville: Thomas Nelson Publishers, 2003.

MacCulloch, J. A. *The Harrowing of Hell.* Edinburgh: T. & T. Clark, 1930.

Madsen, Truman G. *Joseph Smith the Prophet.* Salt Lake City: Bookcraft, 1989.

Matthews, Robert J. *Unto All Nations: A Guide to the Book of Acts and the Writings of Paul.* Salt Lake City: Deseret Book, 1975.

Maxwell, Neal A. *All These Things Shall Give Thee Experience.* Salt Lake City: Deseret Book, 1979.

————. *But for a Small Moment.* Salt Lake City: Bookcraft, 1986.

———. *Even As I Am.* Salt Lake City: Deseret Book, 1982.

———. *Men and Women of Christ.* Salt Lake City: Bookcraft, 1991.

———. *One More Strain of Praise.* Salt Lake City: Bookcraft, 1999.

———. *That My Family Should Partake.* Salt Lake City: Deseret Book, 1974.

———. *A Wonderful Flood of Light.* Salt Lake City: Bookcraft, 1990.

McConkie, Bruce R. *Doctrines of the Restoration: Sermons and Writings of Bruce R. McConkie.* Ed. Mark L. McConkie. Salt Lake City: Bookcraft, 1989.

———. *The Mortal Messiah: The First Coming of Christ.* 4 vols. Salt Lake City: Deseret Book, 1979–81.

———. *A New Witness for the Articles of Faith.* Salt Lake City: Deseret Book, 1985.

———. *The Promised Messiah.* Salt Lake City: Deseret Book, 1978.

McDonald, Lee M. *The Formation of the Christian Biblical Canon.* Rev. ed. Peabody, Mass.: Hendrickson Publishers, 1995.

Messages of the First Presidency of The Church of Jesus Christ of Latter-day Saints. Ed. James R. Clark. 6 vols. Salt Lake City: Bookcraft, 1965–75.

Metzger, Bruce M. *A Textual Commentary on the Greek New Testament.* 2d ed. Stuttgart: United Bible Societies, 1971.

Mosiah: Salvation Only through Christ. Ed. Monte S. Nyman and Charles D. Tate. Provo: BYU Religious Studies Center, 1991.

The New Shorter Oxford English Dictionary on Historical Principles. Ed. Lesley Brown. Oxford: Clarendon Press, 1993.

Nelson, Russell M. *Perfection Pending and Other Favorite Discourses.* Salt Lake City: Deseret Book, 1998.

Nibley, Hugh. *The Message of the Joseph Smith Papyri: An Egyptian Endowment.* Salt Lake City: Deseret Book, 1975.

———. *Mormonism and Early Christianity.* Vol. 4 of *The Collected Works of Hugh Nibley.* Salt Lake City: Deseret Book and FARMS, 1987.

Packer, Boyd K. *The Holy Temple.* Salt Lake City: Bookcraft, 1980.

———. *The Play and the Plan.* Address delivered to a Church Educational System Fireside, 7 May 1995. Salt Lake City: The Church of Jesus Christ of Latter-day Saints, 1995.

Plantinga, Alvin. *God and Other Minds.* Ithaca, N.Y.: Cornell University Press, 1967.

Plain and Precious Truths Restored: The Doctrinal and Historical

Significance of the Joseph Smith Translation. Ed. Robert L. Millet and Robert J. Matthews. Salt Lake City: Bookcraft, 1995.

Pratt, Orson. *The True Faith.* In *A Series of Pamphlets.* Liverpool, 1852.

———. *Orson Pratt's Works.* Comp. Parker Pratt Robinson. Salt Lake City: Deseret News Press, 1945.

Pratt, Parley P. *Autobiography of Parley Parker Pratt.* Ed. Parley P. Pratt Jr. Salt Lake City: Deseret Book, 1976.

———. *Key to the Science of Theology and a Voice of Warning.* Classics in Mormon Literature editon. 2 vols. in 1. Salt Lake City: Deseret Book, 1978.

Priesthood. Salt Lake City: Deseret Book, 1981.

Roberts, B. H. *A Comprehensive History of The Church of Jesus Christ of Latter-day Saints, Century One.* 6 vols. Provo: Brigham Young University Press, 1965.

———. *Defense of the Faith and the Saints.* 2 vols. Salt Lake City: Deseret News, 1907.

———. *Seventy's Course in Theology.* 5 vols. Salt Lake City: Deseret News Press, 1907–12.

Smith, Joseph. *History of The Church of Jesus Christ of Latter-day Saints.* Ed. B. H. Roberts. 2d ed rev. 7 vols. Salt Lake City: The Church of Jesus Christ of Latter-day Saints, 1932—51.

———. *Lectures on Faith.* Salt Lake City: Deseret Book, 1985.

———. *Personal Writings of Joseph Smith.* Ed. Dean C. Jessee. 2d ed. Salt Lake City: Deseret Book, 2002.

———. *Teachings of the Prophet Joseph Smith.* Sel. Joseph Fielding Smith. Salt Lake City: Deseret Book, 1976.

———. *Words of Joseph Smith.* Ed. Andrew F. Ehat and Lyndon W. Cook. Provo, Utah: BYU Religious Studies Center, 1980.

Smith, Joseph F. *Gospel Doctrine: Selections from the Sermons and Writings of Joseph F. Smith.* Salt Lake City: Deseret Book, 1971.

Smith, Joseph Fielding. *Doctrines of Salvation.* Comp. Bruce R. McConkie. 3 vols. Salt Lake City: Bookcraft, 1954–56.

Snow, Lorenzo. *Teachings of Lorenzo Snow.* Ed. Clyde J. Williams. Salt Lake City: Bookcraft, 1996.

Stackhouse, John G., Jr. *Can God Be Trusted? Faith and the Challenge of Evil.* New York: Oxford University Press, 1998.

Swinburne, Richard. *Is There a God?* New York: Oxford University Press, 1996.

Talmage, James E. *Jesus the Christ.* Salt Lake City: Deseret Book, 1972.

Taylor, John. *The Gospel Kingdom: Selections from the Writings and Discourses of John Taylor.* Sel. G. Homer Durham. Salt Lake City: Bookcraft, 1964.

Walker, Charles L. *Diary of Charles L. Walker.* Comp. A. Karl Larson and Catherine Miles Larson. 2 vols. Logan: Utah State University Press, 1980.

Webster, Noah. *An American Dictionary of the English Language.* 1828. Facsimile ed. San Francisco: Foundation for American Christian Education, 1985.

Woodruff, Wilford. *The Discourses of Wilford Woodruff.* Sel. G. Homer Durham. Salt Lake City: Bookcraft, 1946.

Wright, N. T. *The Last Word.* San Francisco: Harper, 2006.

INDEX